Evolving perspectives

ERZIEHUNG IN WISSENSCHAFT UND PRAXIS

Herausgegeben von Johanna Hopfner und Claudia Stöckl

BAND 17

PETER LANG

Zoltán András Szabó / Lajos Somogyvári /
Imre Garai / András Németh (Eds.)

Evolving perspectives

The development of Hungarian educational science after 1945

Editorial Contributor: Bence Ruzsa

PETER LANG
Berlin · Bruxelles · Chennai · Lausanne · New York · Oxford

Library of Congress Cataloging-in-Publication Data
A CIP catalog record for this book has been applied for at the Library of Congress.

Library of Congress Control Number: 2024058976

Bibliographic Information published by the Deutsche Nationalbibliothek
The Deutsche Nationalbibliothek lists this publication in the Deutsche Nationalbibliografie; detailed bibliographic data is available in the internet at http://dnb.d-nb.de.

Cover design by Peter Lang Group AG

Founder's Note
The project has been supported by the National Research Development and Innovation Office (NKFIH/OTKA), grant number: 127937

ISSN 1861-9770
ISBN 978-3-631-91016-0 (Print)
E-ISBN 978-3-631-91017-7 (E-PDF)
E-ISBN 978-3-631-93157-8 (E-PUB)
DOI 10.3726/b22599

Published by Peter Lang GmbH, Berlin (Germany)

info@peterlang.com

This publication has been peer reviewed.

www.peterlang.com

Acknowledgement

Hereby, we would like to thank *László Galántai*, who significantly contributed to the research project with his methodological advice. We would also like to say thank you to *Jamil Toptsi* for his valuable suggestions regarding the text of the book.

Table of Contents

Zoltán András Szabó,[1] Lajos Somogyvári,[2]
Imre Garai,[1] András Németh[1,3]

Hungarian educational science during and after the period of 'actually existing socialism' – a diverse and complex research topic

This volume comprises several papers, summarising a long-term research endeavour conducted between 2018 and 2024. The project, titled '*The past and present of the Hungarian educational science – development of a discipline, scientific communication (1970–2017)*', aimed to examine the development of educational science in the last third of the 20th century and the period following the turn of the millennium. The studies focus on different aspects of socialist pedagogy, including its key figures, the characteristics of their institutional background, and their scientific contributions.

In his essay, **András Németh** offers insight into the research history, focusing on various theoretical and methodological considerations. He begins by presenting a brief history related to the self-reflection of the discipline itself, highlighting the outcomes of significant German workshops and investigations, as well as recent developments in Central and Eastern Europe. The Hungarian research group introduced in this volume continues this discourse, basing its analysis on two theoretical pillars: Rudolf Stichweh's concept of science and an understanding of how totalitarian regimes sacralised politics in the first half of the 20th century, drawing on the works of Emilio Gentile and Carl Voegelin. Utilising archival sources and contemporary publications, the participants concluded that a new phase in Hungarian educational science began in the late 1960s, marking a departure from the trends of previous decades. New scientific infrastructures and socialisation patterns emerged, resulting in the formation of new professional

1 Institute of Education, ELTE Eötvös Loránd University, Budapest, Hungary, nemeth.andras@ppk.elte.hu
2 University of Pannonia, Institute of Education Sciences, Veszprém, Hungary, somogyvari.lajos@htk.uni-pannon.hu
3 Faculty of Teacher Training, J. Selye University, Komárno, Slovakia, nemetha@ujs.sk

communities and scholarly products. The subsequent papers in this volume provide detailed evidence to support this assertion.

The contribution of **Bence Ruzsa, Emese Lukovszki, Beatrix Vincze**, and **Imre Garai**, entitled '*Transformation of the scientific institutional settings of education sciences in the decades after the consolidation of the Kádár-regime*', explores the peculiarities in the formation of the academic institutional base for education in Hungary after 1945. It offers a systematic description of how the elements of the institutional system underwent continuous organisational changes until the 1960s. The research, based on the analysis of archival sources, periodicals, and relevant journals from the period, reveals the position of educational research institutions up until the regime change in 1990, considering the scope afforded by legislation and the educational policy guidelines of the ruling communist party. Furthermore, the study provides insight into the penetration of Marxist-Leninist ideology into the educational structure of scientific universities. The history of the 'college', a communist party-affiliated institution of higher education tasked with training ideological functionaries and embedding itself into the system of higher education institutions, is also introduced in the paper.

The paper '*The recruitment of students in the Party College of the Hungarian Working People's Party (1949–1956)*' authored by **Bence Ruzsa** and **Zoltán András Szabó**, presents a comprehensive historical study of the above-mentioned college-type institution of the party-state dictatorship. The paper outlines the initiatives taken from 1945 to 1948 establishing educational institutions and cultivating an intellectual elite, which were eventually dismantled by Party leadership. The paper explores the vicissitudes and dubious quality of cadre training in the period 1949–1956 (i.e., the frequent organisational changes in the Party College, the year-to-year shifts in admission criteria, and the typical social background characteristics of the student candidates). These are analysed within the social and higher education policy context of the period, employing the methods of historical source analysis, prosopography, and descriptive statistics.

The theoretical concept of political religion offers a novel framework for interpreting various aspects of socialist pedagogy. Marxism-Leninism, as an existing ideology, envisioned a utopia – a parallel world to be achieved by following the ever-changing communist project. When comparing the understanding of Marx in the Socialist Bloc to that of the West, we observe a diametrically opposite, critical philosophy. In their article, **Lajos Somogyvári** and **Zsuzsanna Polyák** analyse the normative imaginaries of Marxism in Hungary, revealing the connection between political religion and socialist pedagogy. The main corpus used in their research utilizes the representative journal of Hungarian educational science,

Magyar Pedagógia (Hungarian Pedagogy). Their survey focused on three main categories – agencies, socio-political imaginaries, and knowledge fields – to reveal how the official ideology influenced different pedagogical genres. Through text mining conducted using MAXQDA software, they found that a small number of authors and specific types of scientific works contained significantly more ideological content than others.

In his paper, **Tibor Darvai** examines the history of educational psychology in Hungary during the 1950s and 1960s. The de-Stalinisation process, initiated by Khrushchev, provided the political impetus for lifting the ban on psychology after 1956 in the Eastern Bloc. This research describes these developments through a specific case study, addressing a key question: Who were the educational psychologists of the Kádár Era? The lead-up to significant change in disciplinary classification began in the late 1950s, when educational psychologists obtained their degrees in educational science. By the 1960s, this trend shifted, with educational psychologists earning their degrees in psychology. As a result, the psychology of education gradually separated from educational science and integrated into the discipline of psychology. This shift also meant that scientific recruitment in educational psychology enriched the field of psychology rather than educational science.

The essay by **Attila Czabaji Horváth**, **Zsófia Albrecht**, **Andrea Daru**, **Dorina Szente**, and **Györgyi Vincze**, titled '*Contributions to the issue of scientific qualification in education in Hungary between 1970 and 1990*', explores the emergence of a new generation of scientists in education during this period. In this context, it examines the system and characteristics of scientific qualification, employing text mining and content analysis to analyse candidates' dissertation abstracts (thesis booklets) in order to understand their topic choices and the knowledge constructions they developed. The analysis also considers how the Scientific-Technological Revolution (STR), a prominent current of the period in question, was represented in the discourse on scientific qualifications. These findings provide important insights into the Soviet-based process of scientific rating and the paths of entry into the scientific field.

The final study by **Erzsébet Golnhofer**, titled '*A moment of autonomy in higher education pedagogy. The Higher Education Pedagogical Academy 1970–1972*', explores how the increasingly open social, political, and scientific environment in Hungary at the end of the 1960s and the beginning of the 1970s, within the framework of the state party, created opportunities for the institutionalisation and autonomy of higher education pedagogy. Employing content analysis of contemporary literature and prosopography, the research examines the expanding institutional frameworks that played an important role in higher education pedagogy, the characteristics of the professionals who developed new knowledge content, the scientific communication network, and the scientific outputs that were generated. The study considers the activities of the Higher Education Pedagogical Research Centre (FPK) and the presentations of the Higher Education Pedagogical Academy (FPA), reviewing how the knowledge elite, willing to adapt to socialist conditions, contributed to the discipline's social recognition. The analyses illustrate the complex, contradictory situation in which higher education pedagogy emerged as an increasingly recognised and independent science, while also bearing the direct and hidden effects of politicisation and ideological expectations from the state party.

András Németh[1,2]

Research history, theoretical background, methodological characteristics

Abstract: Focusing on various theoretical and methodological considerations, this paper provides an overview of the main international trends and achievements in the history of educational research. After a brief historical overview of the discipline's self-reflection, the review also presents the most significant German and other Western European professional workshops and research findings in the field, as well as recent developments in Central and Eastern Europe.

Keywords: research history, education sciences, theoretical background

Introduction

In recent decades, the study of science development within the totalitarian regimes of the 20th century has emerged as a new field of research in the history of education. This includes the exploration of 'Soviet-style' science in former socialist countries and the pedagogical landscapes of communist-socialist dictatorships. Our study volume builds on this line of inquiry, drawing from our prior research on the socialist era of Hungarian educational science (Hopfner et al., 2009; Németh, 2002; Németh et al., 2015; Németh et al., 2016; Németh & Garai, 2019; Németh & Szabolcs, 2021). It synthesises findings from various international and national research projects on the history of education that have recently emerged. Our aim is to provide an overview of significant international research on the history of educational science, outlining their theoretical perspectives, research methods, and key findings. Furthermore, we aim to situate the results of our own research presented in this volume within the broader international academic discourse on the subject.

1 Institute of Education, ELTE Eötvös Loránd University, Budapest, Hungary, nemeth.andras@ppk.elte.hu

2 Faculty of Teacher Training, J. Selye University, Komárno, Slovakia, nemetha@ujs.sk

Aspects of self-reflection in the history of education – a brief historiography of research in the history of science

In the 18th and 19th centuries, when pedagogy began to evolve into a science in the modern sense, there was not yet a recognised need for self-reflection in the history of education. Early historical research in this field centred on timeless concepts of pedagogy, focusing primarily on prominent figures of the era, theological and later philosophical theories of education, and the evolution of schools and educational systems. During the latter half of the 19th century, the primary role of the history of education, as part of university teacher training programmes, was to establish and reinforce professional identity through the introduction of esteemed educators (i.e., canonised classics) (Szabó et al., 2022). By the early 20th century, under the influence of German humanities, there emerged a growing necessity to critically examine the processes of pedagogical scientization, aligning with the theoretical and historical approaches of the time.

These works on the history of ideas, continuing the tradition of the 19th century, represented the life's work of renowned educationalists and were interpreted from a cultural-historical perspective (Heinze, 2021). In the second half of the 20th century, some pedagogically oriented works on the history of science adopted this philosophical and historical perspective (Powell, 1980; Willke, 1975). From the 1970s onwards, there was a shift towards a more differentiated approach that also considered the historical and sociological aspects of scientific development. This strengthening of the sociological and historical approach to science emerged in the social sciences and later in the history of science within educational science. Kuhn and Lakatos, along with Feyerabend's radical critique of science based on historical foundations, were instrumental in this shift. Additionally, the left-wing student movements of the 1960s and Popper's concept of the 'open society' part of the popular liberal theory of society at the time, were also influential.

The theoretical and methodological foundations of this research were laid by the sociology of science developed by Merton, which was based on Talcott Parsons' empirical "structural-functionalist" sociological systems theory of science. Originating in the USA, this approach aimed at fostering a self-understanding of the sciences. The 1970s also saw the development of a strong programme of Anglo-Saxon philosophy and sociology of science known as the "sociology of scientific knowledge" (Barnes et al., 2002), developed in the 1970s under the influence of David Bloor.

One notable European adoption of Parsons and Merton's ideas can be found in the work of German sociologist Niklas Luhmann. The development of the concept of discipline, still widely used in the history of science today, can be traced back to Luhmann's student Rudolf Stichweh (Stichweh, 1984, 1994).

The most important structural elements of this concept include: a) the institutional framework (comprising faculties, departments, and institutes) for conducting science, usually within universities, which operates as a hierarchical body of personnel based on meritocratic principles; b) research work conducted within the context of constantly evolving and renewing theoretical models and concepts, research methodologies, and methodological procedures established by the scientific community in accordance with the organising principles of scientific paradigms; c) the professional communication of research results through scientific publications (e.g., journals, scientific textbooks, and research reports), professional organizations (e.g., scientific societies, associations, and academic communities), and professional events (e.g., networks of scientific conferences); and d) the training of young scientists, which involves the development of legitimate criteria for training and the establishment of a professional socialization and career structure within the discipline, as well as the selection and ideological training (e. g. indoctrination) of young scientists.

The most important constructive element of each discipline in this model is institutionalised communicative relationship among scientists. This component serves to consolidate the research field of the discipline through problem-oriented communicative means, control its social reproduction and communication, and codify the specific knowledge of the discipline as an independent form of expertise (cf. Keiner, 1999).

The socio-historical and sociological works produced between 1970 and 1990s initially focused on the emergence of the academic scientific community and its social role throughout the 20th century (Hornbostel, 1997; Ringer, 1990, 1992; Stehr & Meja, 1981). During this era, the first major summarising monographs, addressing both national development trends and the emergence of pedagogy as an academic discipline, appeared in German and English (Benner, 1973; Böhm & Flores d'Arcais, 1979, 1980; Gosden, 1972; Herbst, 1989; Schriewer, 1983; Schwenk, 1977; Simon, 1994; Speck, 1976; 1978; Thomas, 1990). In addition, there were also efforts to delineate general European and worldwide trends in the development of education science (Depaepe, 1993; Oelkers, 1989; Zedler & König, 1989).

The innovative endeavours in the history of science within the broader field of education science outlined above are most strongly represented in the German research landscape. As part of the German research programme in the history of science, the *Arbeitsgemeinschaft Wissenschaftstheorie und Wissenschaftsforschung* was founded at the end of the 1980s to coordinate the burgeoning research efforts within the *Deutsche Gesellschaft für Erziehungswissenschaft*. In the book series *Beiträge zur Theorie und Geschichte der Erziehungswissenschaft* [Contributions to the Theory and History of Education Science], launched in 1987, more than 20 volumes were published featuring works discussing the results and methodology of the then-emerging research in the history of science in educational science (e.g. Baumert & Roeder, 1990, 1994; Eigler & Magce, 1992, 1994; Herrlitz, 1996).

The most important German workshops on this topic were organised under the direction of Jürgen Schriewer and Heinz-Elmar Tenorth, initially at the University of Frankfurt and later at Humboldt University in Berlin (Keiner, 1999; Schriewer, 1994; Schriewer & Keiner, 1993; Schriewer et al., 1998). These workshops aimed to reconstruct national and international scientific communication networks and, on the basis of international influences and reception processes, to determine the socio-historical context of the development of education science, the relationship between education science and the profession field, content-based internal differentiation processes in the sciences, and the development of its organizational framework, infrastructure, and personnel requirements.

Studies from the 1990s identified the most important developmental trends within the two major models of continental academic development – the French and the German – and laid the groundwork for subsequent research in the second half of the 1990s, which analysed the changes in both the continental and Anglo-Saxon (i.e., British and American) education systems (Keiner & Schriewer 2000; Wagner & Wittrock, 1990). This approach was followed by an international comparative study (Keiner, 1999), which utilised empirical analysis of publications in specialist journals to highlight the differences between the education sciences in the USA, France, Great Britain, and Germany. It also examined the communication processes within the discipline and the particularities of the scientific self-image of the individual countries.

Another strand of German research that began around the millennium examined the personal backgrounds of German university educators, including professors and private lecturers, and the local institutional structure of the discipline (e.g., Horn, 2003). Further work on communication networks detailed how different academic trends, paradigms, networks, and local cultures developed (e.g. Langewand & Prondczynsky, 1999). These works also investigated the thematic and methodological directions of disciplinary change (Macke, 1994), changes in the curricular content of university education (Hauenschild et al., 1993), and its manifestations outside the university context (Horn & Kemnitz, 2002; Rothland, 2008).

In addition, a number of studies on the relationship between education science and the teaching profession, as well as educational policy, were carried out in the years leading up to and following the turn of the millennium (Criblez & Hoffstetter, 2000; Drewek, 1998; Keiner, 1998). Research focusing on the regional characteristics of individual countries was also prominent (Brezinka, 2000, 2003, 2008, 2014; Gautherin, 2002; Hoffstetter & Schneuwly, 2001; 2002; Horn, 2003; Németh, 2002, 2006; Simon, 1994; Tenorth & Horn, 2001).

These international research findings had a significant impact on the development of the theoretical background and methodological tools for our research into the historical development of Hungarian educational science, which began in the late 1990s. Our studies were influenced by the above-mentioned German and Swiss research (e.g., Criblez & Hoffstetter, 2000; Hoffstetter & Schenuwly, 2002; Tenorth & Horn, 2001), which was facilitated through our working relationships with Humboldt University of Berlin and several other German, Austrian and Swiss universities (e.g. Hofstetter & Schneuwly, 2006; Hopfner et al., 2009; Horn et al., 2001).

A new direction of research interest which also influences our research is the pedagogical world of socialist countries in Central and Eastern Europe. In recent decades, a number of German pedagogical historical studies have been undertaken to explore this, focusing primarily on the development of pedagogy in the GDR and various pedagogical fields during the socialist period (Benner & Sladek, 1998; Cloer, 1998; Cloer & Wernstedt, 1994, 1998; Gießler & Wiegmann, 1996; Häder & Tenorth, 1997; Häder & Wiegmann, 2007; Krüger & Marotzki, 1994; Langewellpott 1973; Lost, 2000; Malycha, 2008; Miethe & Weiss, 2020; Tenorth et al., 1996; Tenorth & Wiegmann, 2022; Wiegmann, 2002; Zabel, 2009).

In addition to investigating pedagogical phenomena in the GDR, other former socialist countries have also begun to explore the 'real existing socialism' in education (Donáth, 2006; Golnhofer, 2004, 2006a, 2006b; Kestere & Kruze, 2013; Kestere et al., 2020; Kudlacova & Rajsky, 2019; Pukánszky, 2004; Sáska, 2006; Szabolcs, 2006a, 2006b, 2006c).

Theoretical background and research methodology

This volume summarises the latest findings of our research into the history of Hungarian educational science during the socialist era, utilising the concept of discipline outlined above (Stichweh, 1984, 1994). Due to the political nature of the subject – specifically the Hungarian Rákosi and subsequent Kádár regimes – we also incorporate the concept of political religion as an additional theoretical pillar for our analysis. This concept, introduced by Voegelin, has gained renewed attention for describing 20th century totalitarian regimes (Bärsch, 1997; Faber, 1997; Gentile, 2000, 2001; Harting, 2008; Ley, 1997; Voegelin, 1993).

In his work on the sacralisation of politics, Gentile (2000) defines totalitarian regimes as attempts to seize monopolistic political power by: a) legally or illegally acquiring political power to radically destroy or transform the previous regime, b) establishing a totalitarian one-party state, c) suppressing, integrating, and unifying society as a whole, d) subjecting all individual and collective forms of existence to the political influence of renewal myths, values, and ideologies, and e) attempting to reshape society and all its members through an anthropological revolution, aiming to subordinate all physical and mental manifestations to the revolutionary and imperialist goals of the party to achieve the supranational civilisation that represents the ultimate goal (see Somogyvári et al., 2021).

Building on earlier research, this study explores the specifics of a more recent period, starting with the 1970s and 1980s, just before the regime change, and continuing to examine the development of the educational discipline. It specifically investigates the main socio-political, institutional, and personal relationships of this period. The study examines and analyses the more recent and subtle patterns of institutionalisation processes in contemporary Hungarian society and pedagogy in a narrow sense, as well as the survival and metamorphosis of earlier elements and their impact on the development of social and educational reform processes.

Our initial thesis posits that a new phase in the history of Hungarian socialist pedagogy began at the end of the 1960s, which reorganised many elements of the disciplinary characteristics from the previous decades. These changes laid the groundwork for the radical upheavals within the discipline in the 1980s, leading to the emergence of new scientific infrastructures, socialisation patterns, professional and communicative communities, and new scientific products. The radically unique disciplinary characteristics of socialist education, compared to the Western model of science, along with the 'dormant' structures and networks that continued to function after the transition as well as the patterns of socialisation that persisted as latent and manifest habitus elements, often hindered the development of novel institutional frameworks and content in the new scientific field. This 'inherited' cognitive content frequently impeded far-reaching structural changes, the creation and effective communication of competitive and credible academic products, societal and peer acceptance of the discipline, and the establishment of optimal conditions for the successful professional socialisation of young academics.

Our work draws on a range of archival sources (e.g., materials from universities and ministries and minutes from scientific organisations and events) as well as other literature on the topic (e.g., contemporary scientific book series, textbooks, and journals) identified as part of the research conducted between 2010 and 2024.

We also incorporate partial analyses and case studies from study volumes summarising previous research findings (Garai, 2015, Golnhofer & Szabolcs, 2015; Karády, 2015; Németh et al., 2016; Sáska, 2015; Szabó, 2015). These sources present various aspects of the development of the discipline at the selected locations and institutions, such as university and college departments, research institutes, the academic sphere, and background institutions of the party nomenclature.

The investigations into the cognitive products of education science and its communication processes rely on the databases of domestic educational journals and on partial results of content analyses, which utilise empirical serial data supported by computer software to process data from these journals. A text mining analysis (also known as text analytics) was also carried out as part of the study, which enables the analysis of text corpora in digital format without sampling. In the previous phase of our research, we processed a large number of articles from pedagogical journals; as a result, the entire corpus of *Magyar Pedagógia* [Hungarian Pedagogy] is available alongside other journals.

Bibliography

Barnes, B., Bloor, D., & Henry, J. (2002). *A tudományos tudás szociológiai elemzése.* Osiris Kiadó.

Baumert, J., & Roeder, P. (1990). *Expansion und Wandel der Pädagogik. Zur Institutionalisierung einer Referenzdisziplin.* Max-Planck-Institute.

Baumert J., & Roeder, P. (1994). "Stille Revolution". Zur empirischen Lage der Erziehungswissenschaft. In H.-H. Krüger, & T. Rauschenbach (Eds.), *Erziehungswissenschaft. Die Disziplin am Beginneiner neuen Epoche* (pp. 29–47). Juventa.

Benner, D. (1973). *Hauptströmungen der Erziehungswissenschaft.* Deutscher Studien.

Benner D., & Sladek, H. (1998). Ist Staatspädagogik möglich? Erziehungswissenschaft in SBZ und DDR zwischen Affirmativer Staatspädagogik und reflektierter Pädagogik. In D. Benner, J. Schriewer, & H.-E. Tenorth (Eds.), *Erziehungsstaaten: Historisch-vergleichende Analysen ihrer Denktraditionen und nationaler Gestalten* (pp. 195–224). Deutscher Studien.

Bärsch, C.-E. (1997). *Die politische Religion des Nationalsozialismus.* Wilhelm Fink Verlag.

Böhm, W., & Flores d'Arcais, G. (Eds.). (1979). *Die italienische Pädagogik des 20. Jahrhunderts.* Klett-Cotta.

Böhm, W., & Flores d'Arcais, G. (Eds.). (1980). *Die Pädagogik der frankophonen Länder im 20. Jahrhundert.* Klett-Cotta.

Brezinka, W. (2000). *Pädagogik in Österreich. Die Geschichte des Faches an den Universitäten vom 18. bis zum 20. Jahrhundert* (Vol. 1). Verlag der Österreichischen Akademie der Wissenschaften.

Brezinka, W. (2003). *Pädagogik in Österreich. Die Geschichte des Faches an den Universitäten vom 18. bis zum Ende des 20. Jahrhunderts* (Vol. 2). Verlag der Österreichischen Akademie der Wissenschaften.

Brezinka, W. (2008). *Pädagogik in Österreich: Die Geschichte des Faches an den Universitäten vom 18. bis zum 20. Jahrhundert* (Vol. 3). Verlag der Österreichischen Akademie der Wissenschaften.

Brezinka, W. (2014). *Pädagogik in Österreich. Die Geschichte des Faches an den Universitäten vom 18. bis zum 20. Jahrhundert* (Vol. 4). Verlag der Österreichischen Akademie der Wissenschaft.

Cloer, E., & Wernstedt R. (1994). *Pädagogik in der DDR. Eröffnung einer notwendigen Bilanzierung*. Deutscher Studien.

Cloer, E., & Wernstedt, R. (1998). *Theoretische Pädagogik in der DDR*. Deutscher Studien.

Cloer, E. (1998). *Theoretische Pädagogik in der DDR*. Deutscher Studien.

Criblez, L., & Hoffstetter, R. (Eds.). (2000). *Die Ausbildung von PrimarlehrerInnen. Geschichte und aktuelle Reformen*. Peter Lang.

Depaepe, M. (1993). *Zum Wohl des Kindes? Pädologie, pädagogische Psychologie und experimentelle Pädagogik in Europa und den USA, 1890–1940*. Leuven University Press.

Donáth, P. (2006). "Gyökeres fordulatot a politikai-világnézeti nevelésben". *Educatio, 15*(3), 451– 491. https://epa.oszk.hu/01500/01551/00037/pdf/796.pdf

Drewek, P. (1998). Educational studies as an academic discpline in Germany at the beginning of the 20th century. In P. Drewek, & C. Lüth (Eds.), *History of Educational Studies* (pp. 175–194). C. S. H. P.

Eigler, G., & Magce, G. (1992). *Die Entwicklung der empirischen Forschungsorientierung der Erziehungswissenschaft im Spiegel erziehungswissenschaftlicher Qualifikationsarbeiten*. Deutscher Studien.

Eigler G., & Magce, G. (1994). *Wissenschaftstheorie und erziehungswissenschaftliche Forschungspraxis*. Deutscher Studien.

Faber, R. (Eds.). (1997). *Politische Religion – Religiöse Politik*. Königshausen & Neumann.

Garai, I. (2015). Tudománypolitika és felsőoktatás Magyarországon, 1948–1951. In A. Németh, Zs. H. Biró, & I. Garai (Eds.): *Neveléstudomány és tudományos elit a 20. század második felében*. (pp. 165–176), Gondolat Kiadó.

Gautherin, J. (2002). *Une discipline pour la République: La Science de l'éducation en France 1882–1914*. Peter Lang.

Gentile, E. (2000). Die Sakralisierung der Politik - Einige Definitionen, Interpretationen und Reflexionen. In H. Maier (Ed.), *Wege in die Gewalt - Die modernen politischen Religionen* (pp. 166–182). Fischer Taschenbuch.

Gentile, E. (2001). *Le religioni della politica: Fra democrazie e totalitarismi.* Laterza.

Gießler, G., & Wiegmann, U. (1996). *Pädagogik und Herrschaft in der DDR: Die parteilichen, geheimdienstlichen und vormilitärischen Erziehungsverhältnisse.* Peter Lang.

Golnhofer, E. (2004). *Hazai pedagógiai nézetek 1945–1949.* Iskolakultúra. http://misc.bibl.u-szeged.hu/45489/1/iskolakultura_konyvek_023.pdf

Golnhofer, E. (2006a). Rendszerváltások a tudomány legitimációjában – Magyarország, 1945–1949. In É. Szabolcs (Ed.), *Pedagógia és politika a XX. század második felében Magyarországon* (pp. 9–28). Eötvös József Könyvkiadó.

Golnhofer, E. (2006b). Rendszerváltások és egyéni élettörténetek. *Educatio, 15*(3), 539–552. https://epa.oszk.hu/01500/01551/00037/pdf/799.pdf

Golnhofer E., & Szabolcs É. (2015). Szempontok egy elfelejtett diskurzus értelmezéséhez: a Petőfi Kör pedagógusvitája. In G. Baska & J. Hegedűs (Eds.): *Égi iskolák, földi műhelyek* (pp. 359–370). ELTE PPK.

Gosden, P. H. J. H. (1972). *The Evolution of a Profession: A Study of the Contribution of Teachers' Associations to the Development of School Teaching as a Professional Occupation.* Blackwell.

Hauenschild, H., Herrlitz, H.-G. & Kruse, B. (1993). *Die Lehrgestalt der westdeutschen Erziehungswissenschaft von 1945 bis 1990 (LEWERZ)* (Göttinger Beiträge zur erziehungswissenschaftlichen Forschung No. 6/7). Pädagogisches Seminar der Georg-August-Universität Göttingen. https://doi.org/10.47952/gro-publ-160

Häder, S., & Tenorth, H.-E. (Eds.). (1997). *Bildungsgeschichte einer Diktatur.* Deutscher Studien.

Häder, S., & Wiegmann, U. (Eds.). (2007). *Die Akademie der Pädagogischen Wissenschaften der DDR im Spannungsfeld von Wissenschaft und Politik.* Peter Lang.

Harting, A. (2008). *Verheißung und Erlösung. Religion und ihre weltlichen Ersatzbildungen in Politik und Wissenschaft.* Passagen Verlag.

Krüger, H.-H., & Marotzki, W. (Eds.). (1994). *Pädagogik und Erziehungsalltag in der DDR.* Leske und Budrich.

Heinze, C. (2021). Erziehungswissenschaft und pädagogisches Wissen. In G. Kluchert, K.-P. Horn, K. Groppe, & M. Caruso (Eds.), *Historische Bildungsforschung: Konzepte - Methoden - Forschungsfelder* (pp. 365–372). Julius Klinkhardt.

Herbst, J. (1989). *And Sadly Teach: Teacher Education and Professionalization in American Culture*. University of Wisconsin Press.

Herrlitz, H.-G. (1996). Kontinuität und Wandel der erziehungswissenschaftlichen Lehrgestalt. Materialien zur Analyse des Lehrangebots westdeutscher Universitäten 1945/46–1989. In A. Leschinsky (Ed.), *Die Institutionalisierung von Lehren und Lernen Beiträge zu einer Theorie der Schule* (pp. 265–282). Beltz. https://www.pedocs.de/volltexte/2014/9802/pdf/Herrlitz_1996_Kontinuitaet_und_Wandel_der_erziehungswissenschaftlichen_Lehrgestalt.pdf

Hofstetter, R., & Schneuwly, B. (Eds.). (2001). *Le pari des sciences de l'éducation*. De Boeck Supérieur.

Hofstetter, R., & Schneuwly, B. (Eds.). (2002). *Erziehungswissenschaft(en) 19–20. Jahrhundert. Zwischen Profession und Disziplin*. Peter Lang.

Hofstetter, R., & Schneuwly, B. (Eds.). (2006). *Passion, Fusion, Tension. New Education and Educational Sciences*. Peter Lang.

Hornbostel, S. (1997). *Wissenscahftsindikatoren. Bewertung in der Wissenschaft*. Verlag für Sozialwissenschaften. DOI: https://doi.org/10.1007/978-3-322-90335-8.

Hopfner, J., Németh, A., & Szabolcs, É. (Eds.). (2009). *Kindheit – Schule-Erziehungswissenschaft in Mitteleuropa 1948–2008*. Peter Lang.

Horn, K.-P. (2003). *Erziehungswissenschaft in Deutschland im 20. Jahrhundert*. Julius Klinkhardt.

Horn, K.-P., & Kemnitz, H. (Eds.). (2002). *Pädagogik unter den Linden. Von der Gründung der Berliner Universität im Jahre 1810 bis zum Ende des 20. Jahrhunderts*. Steiner.

Horn, K-P., Németh, A., Pukánszky B., & Tenorth, H-E. (Eds.). (2001). *Erziehungswissenschaft in Mitteleuropa: Aufklärerische Traditionen – deutscher Einfluss – nationale Eigenständigkeit*. Gondolat Kiadó.

Karády V. (2015). Egy szocialista értelmiségi „államnemesség"? Kandidátusok és akadémiai doktorok a hazai társadalomtudományokban. In A. Németh, Zs. H. Biró, & I. Garai (Eds.): *Neveléstudomány és tudományos elit a 20. század második felében* (pp. 251–281). Gondolat Kiadó.

Keiner, D. (1998). *Erziehungswissenschaft und Bildungspolitik*. Peter Lang.

Keiner, E. (1999). *Erziehungswissenschaft 1947–1990: Eine empirische und vergleichende Untersuchung zur kommunikativen Praxis einer Disziplin*. Deutscher Studien.

Keiner, E., & Schriewer, J. (2000). Erneuerung aus dem Geist der eigenen Tradition? Über Kontinuität und Wandel nationaler Denkstile in der Erziehungswisenschaft. *Schweizerische Zeitschrift für Bildungswissenschaften, 22*(1), 27–50. https://doi.org/10.24452/sjer.22.1.5078

Kestere, I., & Kruze, A. (Eds.). (2013). *History of Pedagogy and Educational Sciences in the Baltic Countries from 1940 to 1990*. RaKa.

Kestere, I., Sarv, E.-S., & Stonkuviene, I. (Eds.). (2020). *Pedagogy and Educational Sciences in the Post-Soviet Baltic States, 1990–2004: Changes and Challenges*. University of Latvia Press.

Kudlacova, B., & Rajsky, A. (Eds.). (2019). *Education and "Pädagogik". Philosophical and Historical Reflections (Central, Southern and South-Eastern Europe)*. Peter Lang.

Langewand, A., & Prondczynsky A. (Eds.). (1999). *Lokale Wissenschaftskulturen in der Erziehungswissenschaft*. Deutscher Studienverlag.

Langewellpott, Ch. (1973). *Erziehungswissenschaft und pädagogische Praxis in der DDR. Zwei wissenschaftstheoretische Modelle 1945–1952*. Schwann.

Ley, M. (1997). *Der Nationalsozialismus als politische Religion*. Philo.

Lost, C. (2000). *Sowjetpädagogik: Wandlungen, Wirkungen, Wertungen in der Geschichte der DDR*. Schneider.

Macke, G. (1994). Disziplinärer Wandel. Erziehungswissenschaft auf dem Wege zur Verselbständigung ihrer Teildisziplinen. In H.-H. Krüger & Th. Rauschenbach (Eds.), *Erziehungswissenschaft. Die Disziplin am Beginn einer neuen Epoche* (pp. 49–68). Deutscher Studien Verlag.

Malycha, A. (2008). *Die Akademie der Pädagogischen Wissenschaften der DDR 1970–1990*. Akademische Verlagsanstalt.

Miethe, I., & Weiss, J. (Eds.). (2020). *Socialist Education Cooperation and the Global South*. Peter Lang.

Németh, A. (2002). *A magyar neveléstudomány fejlődéstörténete*. Gondolat Kiadó.

Németh, A. (2006). The relationship between educational science at the universities and educational movements influenced by "new education" outside academia In R. Hofstetter, & B. Schneuwly (Eds.), *Passion, Fusion, Tension. New Education and Educational Sciences* (pp. 169–190). Peter Lang.

Németh, A., & Garai, I. (2019). Disciplinary changes in the Hungarian Pädagogik from the second half of the 19th century to the collapse of Stalinist-type dictatorship. In B. Kudláčová, & A. Rajský (Eds.), *Education and "Pädagogik" – Philosophical and historical reflections: Central, Southern and South-Eastern Europe* (pp. 210–229). Peter Lang. https://doi.org/10.3726/b15688

Németh, A., & Szabolcs, É. (2021). Educational Science as an Academic Discipline in Hungary (1867–1953): Turns and Developmental Phases. In S. Van Ruyskensvelde, G. Thyssen, F. Herman, A. Van Gorp, & P. Verstraete (Eds.), *Folds of Past, Present and Future: Reconfiguring Contemporary Histories of Education* (pp. 249–266). De Gruyter Oldenbourg. https://doi.org/10.1515/9783110623451-014

Németh, A., Biró, Zs. H., & Garai, I. (Eds.). (2015). *Neveléstudomány és tudományos elit a 20. század második felében*. Gondolat Kiadó.

Németh, A., Garai, I., & Szabó, Z. A. (Eds.). (2016). *Neveléstudomány és pedagógiai kommunikáció a szocializmus időszakában*. Gondolat Kiadó.

Oelkers, J. (1989). *Die grosse Aspiration: Zur Herausbildung der Erziehungswissenschaft im 19. Jahrhundert*. Wissenschaftliche Buchgesellschaft.

Powell, A. G. (1980). *The Uncertain Profession: Harvard and the Search for Educational authority*. Harvard University Press.

Pukánszky, B. (2004). Schulpolitische Debatten während der Oktoberrevolution in Ungarn 1956. In S. Häder, & U. Wiegmann (Eds.), *„Am Rande des Bankrotts..." Intellektuelle und Pädagogik in Gesellschaftkrisen der Jahre 1953, 1956 und 1968 in der DDR, Ungarn und der ČSSR* (pp. 93–106). Schneider.

Ringer, F. K. (1990). *The Decline of the German Mandarins. The German Academic Community, 1890–1933*. Wesleyan University Press.

Ringer, F. K. (1992). *Fields of Knowledge. French Academic Culture in Comparative Perspective, 1890–1920*. Cambridge University Press.

Rothland, M. (2008). *Disziplingeschichte in Kontext. Erziehungswissenschaft an der Universität Munster nach 1945*. Klinkhardt.

Stehr, N., & Meja, V. (1981). Wissen und Gesellschaft. *Kölner Zeitschrift für Soziologie und Sozialpsychologie, Sonderheft 22*, 9–19.

Sáska, G. (2006). A társadalmi egyenlőség megteremtésének kísérlete az ötvenes évek felsőoktatásában. *Educatio, 15*(3), 593–608. https://epa.oszk.hu/01500/01551/00037/pdf/802.pdf

Sáska, G. (2015). A neveléstudományi elit viszonya a politikai marxizmushoz az ötvenes években. In A. Németh, Zs. H. Biró, & I. Garai (Eds.). *Neveléstudomány és tudományos elit a 20. század második felében* (pp. 177–212). Gondolat Kiadó.

Schriewer, J. (1983). Pädagogik - ein deutsches Syndrom? Universitäre Erziehungswissenschaft in deutsch-französischen Vergleich. *Zeitschrift für Pädagogik, 29*(3), 359–361. https://doi.org/10.25656/01:14260

Schriewer, J. (1994). *Welt-System und Interrelations-Gefüge. Die Internationalisierung der Pädagogik als Problem Vergleichender Erziehungswissenschaft*. Humboldt-Universität zu Berlin.

Schriewer, J., Henze, J., Wichmann, J., Knost, P., Taubert, J., & Barucha, S. (1998). Konstruktion von internationalität: Referenzhorizonte pädagogischen wissens im wandel gesellschaftlicher systeme (Spanien, Sowjetunion/Russland, China). In H. Kaelble, & J. Schriewer (Eds.), *Gesellschaften im Vergleich. Forschungen aus Sozial und Geschichtswissenschaften* (pp. 151–258). Peter Lang.

Schriewer, J., & Keiner, E. (1993). Kommunikationsnetze und Theoriegestalt. Zur Binnenkonstitution der Erziehungswissenschaft in Frankreich und Deutschland. In J. Schriewer, E. Keimer, & C. Charle (Eds.), *Sozialer Raum und akademische Kulturen* (pp. 277–341). Peter Lang.

Schwenk, B. (1977). Pädagogik in den philosophischen Fakultäten – Zur Entstehungsgeschichte der „geisteswissenschaftlichen" Pädagogik in Deutschland. In H. D. Haller, & D. Lenzen (Eds.), *Wissenschaft im Reformprozeß, Aufklärung oder Alibi?* (pp. 103–131). Klett-Cotta.

Simon, B. (1994). The study of education as a university subject in Britain. In B. Simon (Ed.), *The State and Educational Change: Essays in the History of Education and Pedagogy* (pp. 128–145). Lawrence & Wishart.

Somogyvári, L., Polyák, Zs., & Németh, A. (2021). Új elméleti keretek a szocialista neveléstudomány vizsgálatára: A politikai vallás. *Magyar Pedagógia, 121*(1), 85–97. https://doi.org/10.17670/MPed.2021.1.85

Speck, J. (Ed.). (1976). *Problemgeschichte der neueren Pädagogik* (Vol. 1–3). Kohlhammer.

Speck, J. (Ed.). (1978). *Geschichte der Pädagogik des 20. Jahrhunderts* (Vol. 1–2). Kohlhammer.

Stichweh, R. (1984). *Zur Entstehung des modernen Systems wissenschaftlicher Disziplinen: Physik in Deutschland, 1740–1890.* Suhrkamp.

Stichweh, R. (1994). *Wissenschaft, Universität, Professionen.* Suhrkamp.

Szabó, Z. A. (2015). Hálózat – tudomány – történet. In A. Németh, Zs. H. Biró, & I. Garai (Eds.), *Neveléstudomány és tudományos elit a 20. század második felében* (pp. 83–111). Gondolat Kiadó.

Szabó, Z. A., Garai, I., & Németh, A. (2022). The history of education in Hungary from the mid-19th century to present day. *Paedagogica Historica, 58*(6), 901–919. https://doi.org/10.1080/00309230.2022.2090849

Szabolcs, É. (2006a). Az 1956-os balatonfüredi pedagóguskonferencia. In É. Szabolcs (Ed.), *Pedagógia és politika a XX. század második felében Magyarországon* (pp. 165–177). Eötvös József Könyvkiadó.

Szabolcs, É. (Ed.). (2006b). *Pedagógia és politika a XX. század második felében Magyarországon.* Eötvös József Könyvkiadó.

Szabolcs, É. (2006c). „Pedagógiánk… valóban népünk nevelőihez fog szólni". *Educatio, 15*(3), 609–622. https://epa.oszk.hu/01500/01551/00037/pdf/803.pdf

Tenorth, H.-E., & Horn, K.-P. (2001): Erziehungswissenschaft in Deutschland in der ersten Hälfte des 20. Jahrhunderts. In K.-P. Horn, A. Németh, B. Pukánszky, & H.-E. Tenorth (Eds.), *Erziehungswissenschaft in Mitteleuropa. Aufklärerische Traditionen – deutscher Einfluß – nationale Eigenständigkeit* (pp. 176–191). Osiris Kiadó.

Tenorth, H.-E., & Wiegmann, U. (2022). *Pädagogische Wissenschaft in der DDR*. Julius Klinkhardt.

Tenorth, H.-E., Kudella, S., & Paetz, A. (1996). *Politisierung der Schulalltag der DDR*. Deutscher Studien.

Thomas, J. B. (Ed.). (1990). *British Universities and Teacher Education: A Century of Change*. Falmer Press.

Voegelin, E. (1993). *Die politischen Religionen*. Bermann-Fischer.

Wagner, P., & Wittrock, B. (1990). States, Institutions and Discourses: A Comparative Perspective on the Structuralisation on the Social Sciences. In P. Wagner, B. Wittrock, & R. Whitley (Eds.), *Discourses on Society. The Shaping of the Social Science Disciplines* (pp. 331–357). Kluwer Academic Publishers.

Wiegmann, U. (2002). Robert Alt und Heinrich Deiters. Die Anfänge universitären sozialisticher Pädagogik und Lehrerbildung. In K.-P. Horn, & H. Kemnitz (Eds.), *Pädagogik unter den Linden: von der Gründung der Berliner Universität im Jahre 1810 bis zum Ende des 20. Jahrhunderts* (pp. 253–270). Franz Steiner.

Willke, I. (1975). *Läroskolar i pedagogik vid europeiska universitet*. Almquist & Wiksell.

Zabel, N. (2009). *Zur Geschichte des Deutschen Pädagogischen Zentralinstituts der DDR. Eine institutionsgeschichtliche Studie*. Dissertation. Philosophischen Fakultät der Technischen Universität Chemnitz. https://d-nb.info/1002480337/34

Zedler, P., & König, E. (Eds.). (1989). *Rekonstruktionen pädagogischer Wissenschaftsgeschichte*. Deutscher Studien Verlag.

Bence Ruzsa,[1] Emese Lukovszki,[1] Beatrix Vincze,[2] Imre Garai[2]

Transformation of the scientific institutional settings of education sciences in the decades after the consolidation of the Kádár-regime

Abstract: In the decades following the consolidation of the Kádár regime, the scientific institutional settings of education sciences underwent remarkable change. The process of separating research and teaching activities culminated in a divergent institutional landscape. By applying Rudolf Stichweh's theory on the development of scientific disciplines, institutional transformation is examined across four research aspects. Three main groups of institutions are examined to depict the background of the transformation, namely traditional universities, newly established research institutions, and politically-affiliated entities. The chronological boundaries consist of three major turning points in the cultural and education policy of the Kádár-regime in 1961, 1972, and 1985. A document analysis of archival sources from the investigated institutions, hermeneutic analysis, and a review of secondary literature were employed as primary methods. The results suggest that the Kádár regime continued to follow the reforms begun in the early 1950s to separate scientific research from teaching activities, enabling the regime to exert unconditional control over the scientific field. Marxism-Leninism, as an ideological subject, provided a cohesive force that enabled the exercise of authority over the sciences. In training Marxist-Leninist experts, the Political Academy played a pivotal role, initially operating as a political institution but later adopting some attributes of scientific institutions. By separating research activities from teaching, the communist party achieved its long-anticipated goal of eradicating the remnants of the Humboldtian ideal of university training. The divergent institutional system had a long-lasting effect on the education sciences that can be felt even today.

Keywords: education sciences, Marxism-Leninism, divergent institutional system, Kádár regime, Humboldtian ideal, socialist ideal of scientific research

1 Doctoral School of Education, ELTE Eötvös Loránd University, Budapest, Hungary, ruzsa.bence@ppk.elte.hu; emese.lukovszki@gmail.com

2 Institute of Education, ELTE Eötvös Loránd University, Budapest, Hungary, vincze.beatrix@ppk.elte.hu; garai.imre@ppk.elte.hu

Introduction

In our paper, we investigate the institutional system of education sciences in Hungary between 1960 and 1990 with a focus on the following aspects: the role of education sciences in university training, how the institutional background of the discipline changed over time, and its role in the Political Academy (PA) of the Central Committee (CC) of the Hungarian Socialist Workers' Party (*Magyar Szocialista Munkáspárt*, hereafter MSZMP). During the investigation, changes in the institutional settings of the discipline are revealed through the analysis of archival sources and relevant secondary literature.

As for the result of the research, it can be claimed that education sciences played a role in training education scientists and pedagogues. Nevertheless, research capacity concentrated in research institutions that emerged in parallel with universities as a result of political developments. The communist party demanded research results from these institutions that could be utilised in political decision-making, particularly in regard to youth policy and the long-term development of the education system. Universities and research institutions were often criticised if their research activities were not focused on key areas the party deemed crucial, and therefore they did not provide research materials to support the decision-making process. In connection with the PA, it was found that this institution followed the formal criterion for the operation of regular universities, and even education departments were operated within it. This particular department trained propagandists and contributed to the education of Marxist-Leninist lecturers at universities by conveying knowledge related to school pedagogy and methodology.

By examining the institutional changes of the discipline, the process by which research and teaching-related activities were separated from each other in the field of education sciences could be revealed. This prolonged separation during the decades of socialism contributed to the abolition of the Humboldtian university model in Hungary.

Given the frequent use of the term 'education sciences' in this paper, it is important to define it. The scope and representatives of education sciences were clearly delineated after the implementation of Soviet-style university training in 1949 for ideological reasons. As a result of the reform, 'pedagogy' as an individual subject appeared in the training of scientific researchers in the field of education.[3]

3 National Archives of Hungary (NAH) XIX-I-h, Box 249, 1400–52, 1950–1951. Introduction of the single-subject teacher training and the relocation of the Geography Department. Budapest, June 19, 1951.

In this way, 'pedagogy' was understood as both a practical pursuit as well as a scientific discipline. For the latter sense, 'education sciences' is used as a key term in this paper. Education sciences at that time incorporated the history of education, general psychology, theory of education, general didactics, the psychology of education, and special didactics of secondary school subjects.[4] In the Kádár-era, education sciences blended historical and comparative pedagogy, organisational studies of education institutions, the theory of education and learning, pedagogy across different levels of education (from kindergarten education to university training), pedagogy of socio-cultural institutions (e.g., museum pedagogy or military pedagogy), and the didactics of secondary school subjects (Németh & Biró, 2016, pp. 97–101). Education scientists could be separated into two distinct groups. The first group transformed the ideology of the party with teleological intentions into research aims within the discipline. Within this group, there were overlaps between politicians and education researchers, as some politicians converted their political capital into scientific capital. Members of the second group consisted of those individuals who obtained their qualifications in the new quasi-research institutions modelled after traditional universities. Their main task was to transmit the ideology of the party within regular education institutions (Németh & Biró, 2016, pp. 79–81).

In recent decades, increasing attention has been paid to investigating the history of education as a subdiscipline and its scientific outcomes. These investigations have brought the history of education sciences into the forefront of this field of research. This trend resulted in numerous international (Hopfner et al., 2009; Horn, 2003; Kudlacová & Rajsky, 2019) as well as Hungarian papers and volumes (Németh et al., 2015; Németh et al., 2016; Szabolcs, 2006), with several works focused on developments in education sciences or, more broadly, on shifts in education affairs after 1945 (Darvai, 2021; Golnhofer, 2004; Golnhofer & Szabolcs, 2020; Somogyvári, 2021).

Our paper aligns with this latter research direction by examining the network of research institutions in the education sciences between 1960 and 1989. It focuses on three main education policy reforms of the Kádár-era: the 3rd Act of 1961, the Education Declarations of the CC, and the 1st Act of 1985; these pivotal points serve as milestones which help to divide this time into distinct periods. This periodical division reveals the role that education sciences played in university

4 NAH XIX-I-1-h, Box 336, 1416-1-147, 1949. 1416–15. Bodolay, Géza: Pedagogical lectures for students of the philosophy and nature sciences faculties. Budapest, August 23, 1949.

training and how research institutions became seperate from the broader academic sphere. The selection of these periodical cornerstones is justified by the transformative effect that these reforms had on university training and research institutions due to the remarkable interplay between the political-economic and social developments (Kelemen, 2003).

This paper is a result of a research project aimed at unveiling the disciplinary development of education sciences. Its theoretical foundations lay in the discipline theory of Rudolf Stichweh, who identified four components of discipline involvement. The first comprises the historical development of a research area and the professionalisation of its research activities, including its institutionalisation.[5] The second aspect is the occurrence of professional communication networks. The third is tied to the products of scientific research programs that address social challenges. Lastly, a discipline requires institutionalised training to supply and educate young researchers. This training must convey the accumulated theoretical knowledge of the scientific community in question (Németh, 2015, pp. 64–65).

Utilising the above components, our analysis first examined how the staff of the institutions (both universities and separate research institutions) within the educational sciences changed. Secondly, we investigated how institutions and their inner structures were modified as a result of political shifts. The third aspect of our research is concerned with the connections between disciplinary institutions and state-affiliated organisations. The last analytical perspective is focused on revealing the theoretical underpinnings that guided research activities and their cognitive outcomes. Our paper presents these findings in relation to the changes that occurred within the institutional network of educational sciences as well as the connections between state organisations and the research conducted by quasi-scientific institutions.[6]

5 Within the research project, the Group for investigating the institutional settings of education sciences is comprised of the following members: Andrea Daru, Imre Garai, Ádám Horváth, Emese Lukovszki, András Németh, Mária Persa, Bence Ruzsa, Janka Tresó-Balogh, Beatrix Vincze. The authors of this paper are grateful for their efforts in obtaining archival sources. The research phase and the analysis of the archival sources are led by Imre Garai as the head of this part of the research project.

6 The adjective of "quasi" alludes here to the fact that Marxism penetrated into the core of sciences, particularly humanities, which resulted in the transformation into quasi-scientific disciplines. Criteria regarding the operation of the scientific field were preserved formally, but scholars were expected to produce scientific results in line with the policy of the state party. This expectation compromised the way scientific disciplines operated in the long term.

Given that the research questions are aimed at uncovering the unique mechanisms of the decision-making process of the state party and the social context in which the scientific institutions operate, it is essential to involve multiple layers of sources in the research. Education and higher education policy related to education sciences were examined using the archival materials of the Political Committee (PC)[7] and the CC,[8] which functioned as a forum for confronting the ideas of various social and interest groups (Kalmár, 1998, p. 20). Additionally, materials from the party Secretary were also analysed.[9]

Analysing the archival materials from various party organisations enabled us to understand the administrative decision-making processes affecting the social-political context of education sciences (and sciences in general). Similar materials were discovered in connection with the PA[10] and the Pedagogical Research Group (PRG) of the Hungarian Academy of Sciences (HAS).[11] Among higher education institutions, yearbooks and other types of informational documents from four universities[12] were examined to explore disciplinary changes of education sciences: the universities of Budapest,[13] Szeged (Ketskeméty et al., 1996), Debrecen (Orosz & Barta, 2012) and Pécs (Lengvári & Polyák, 2017). Secondary sources were also involved in the research, aiding in contextualising the findings from the perspectives of both the history of education and general history.

During the analysis of the sources, three traditional methods were employed. The first was the documentary analysis of archival sources (Kéri, 2001, pp. 60–64; Szabolcs, 2011, pp. 84–94), which involved the preparation of short extracts (registers) about the content of the sources (Simon, 1963). The second method, hermeneutic analysis, was also utilised to reveal the latent elements within the source content (Wernet, 2014), which allowed for a dialectical synthesis (see Kéri, 2001, p. 73). In this way, historical processes unveiled by the investigation of the sources

---

7 NAH Fonds 288, u. 5/356. – F. 288, u. 5/1079.

8 NAH F. 288, u. 4/73–74. – F. 288, u. 4/264/265.

9 NAH F. 288, u. 7/152. – F. 288, u. 7/805.

10 NAH F. 288, u. 5/443, F. 288, u. 7/321., F. 288, u. 59/1., Periodicals of "Pártélet" [Life within the Party] and "Politikai Főiskola Közleményei" [Journal of the Political Academy] have also been processed during the investigation.

11 Archive of the Hungarian Academy of Sciences (AHAS). III. Box 227, V. Box 241., XII. 705. Box 53., Box 55.

12 Thus the history of pedagogy colleges responsible for training elementary teachers are excluded from the current investigation.

13 Az Eötvös Loránd Tudományegyetem értesítői [Yearbooks of Eötvös Loránd University], 1959/1960–1988/1989. https://edit.elte.hu/xmlui/handle/10831/60/browse?rpp=20&sort_by=1&type=title&offset=60&etal=-1&order=ASC

were contextualised within the general socio-historical framework of the examined period through the involvement of secondary sources and the application of the theoretical concepts of Stichweh and Bourdieu. Thus, inspected historical phenomena could be understood not only through the examination of sources but also through a system of theoretical notions during the interpretation which were not directly attached to the investigated historical developments (Betti, 1992, pp. 19–21; Kéri, 2001, pp. 72–73).

The third method employed in our research was a secondary literature review, which aided in the contextualisation of the findings within the historical scope of the education sciences discipline and general history. Thus, it contributed to achieving the previously mentioned dialectical synthesis by uncovering data and inferences not mentioned in our primary sources (Coffey, 2014). Additionally, it also assisted in situating the development of the education sciences within the transformation of Hungarian higher education and the shifts in the imperial policy of the Soviet Union (Kalmár, 2014, pp. 187–202; Rainer, 2011a).

Guidelines for education and science policy

The development of an ideological, scientific, and cultural direction in line with the political practice of the MSZMP was achieved through the teaching of Marxism-Leninism. In 1958, the PC issued new cultural policy guidelines that could be interpreted as a caesura, including key elements for the reorganisation and modernisation of the cultural and educational sectors (see Table 1, Kalmár, 1998, p. 158). The PC welcomed the people's democratic reform, which transformed the characteristics of the universities from the Horthy regime and introduced compulsory education in Marxism-Leninism, laying the foundations for scientific ideological training for students. According to the record, training was determined by two factors: the activity of existing Marxist specialists and the presence of ideology, as well as the definition of appropriate methodological principles for the lecturers. These elements collectively aimed to improve the quality of university education and provided guidelines for further improvement in ideological, political, and moral training in higher education.[14] In the second half of the 1950s, the role of science in building socialism increased (especially in fields such as philosophy, history, and later economics and nuclear science). The party expected the social sciences to address current political issues and provide a basis for long-term decision-making (Kalmár, 1998, p. 168–170).

---

14 NAH F. 288, u. 5/69. 79–226. Report about the session of the PC. Budapest, March 11, 1958.

In 1961, the 22nd Congress of the Communist Party of the Soviet Union (CPSU) acknowledged the growing role of science in production and social organisation, heralding the dawn of a new era for mankind: the scientific and technological revolution. This was based on the recognition that, in addition to the establishment of new production structures, the training of a skilled, differentiated, well-educated, self-motivated, and involved workforce was essential for the construction and development of socialism. In line with this declaration, the 3rd Act of 1961 emphasised the role of science in production. Its aim was to increase the number of participants in education and higher education, to support outstanding individuals to become researchers, and to train Marxist-Leninist specialists. This highlighted the dual focus on training young professionals and the ideological aspects present in all disciplines during the selection process. In the spirit of the concepts of the 'scientification of production' and 'industrialisation of science', both basic and applied research, along with teaching and training, were to serve economic purposes in collaboration with enterprises (Kalmár, 2014, pp. 185–187).

In 1972, the PC was fundamentally critical of higher education institutions, questioning them for failing to implement the party's science policy directives despite their development into scientific centres. They criticised academics for not keeping pace with developments and highlighted the lack of university lecturers with relevant theoretical and practical experience, while also identifying the overloaded and unrealistic curricula as a major obstacle to ideological and political training. Shortcomings were also described in connection with moral education.[15] Further problems were also diagnosed, such as inefficient, uncoordinated research activities that were barely linked to other disciplines, and the lack of experimental pedagogy and schools. The PC's primary objectives were to improve research, to study and find solutions to current problems in teaching, and lay the groundwork for long-term decision-making in educational policy. Other objectives were to increase research development opportunities, utilise existing resources more effectively, appoint university and college faculty for fixed-term positions, and provide a greater role for research staff in teaching as a part of inter-institutional cooperation. According to their guidelines, the role of higher education was to provide core education, while the training of specialists was to be carried out in various additional programmes.[16] As a result of the separation of research and

---

15 NAH F. 288, u. 4/117–118. 310–313. Report about the session of the PC. Budapest, 14–15 July 1972.

16 NAH F. 288, u. 4/117–118. 322–323. Report about the session of the PC. Budapest, 14–15 July 1972.

studies, the PC's decisions abolished the remnants of the Humboldtian model of higher education.

The 1st Act of 1985 on education declared that the task of higher education was the training of socialist intellectuals with a scientific profile and encouraging cooperation with enterprises as well as other institutions of higher education, research, and training. It also regulated the acquisition of academic degrees and defined the training of young researchers as part of postgraduate education. Furthermore, the act granted universities greater autonomy in determining their research focuses (Polónyi & Kozma, 2020, p. 504).

Table 1: Formation of the Ministry of Public Education (own editing)

Name of the Ministry (in English and in Hungarian)	Period of operation
Ministry of Religion and Public Education Vallás- és Közoktatásügyi Minisztérium	1867 (1919)–1951
Ministry of Public Education Közoktatásügyi Minisztérium	1951–1953
Ministry of Higher Education Felsőoktatási Minisztérium	1952–1953
Ministry of Education Oktatásügyi Minisztérium	1953–1957
Ministry of Cultural Affairs Művelődésügyi Minisztérium	1957–1974
Ministry of Education Oktatásügyi Minisztérium	1974–1980
Ministry of Cultural Affairs Művelődési Minisztérium	1980–1990

Universities

Establishment of Marxist-Leninist departments

After World War II, Hungarian communist forces sought to transform public and higher education in the spirit of Marxism-Leninism (Horváth, 2016).[17] Ideological subjects became central to university curricula: starting in 1947 with 'The principles of Marxism', followed by the introduction of Political economy, Labour

17 Study and examination regulations of the Faculty of Evangelical Theology of the University of Pécs [Issued by Ministerial Decree No. 3650/1947 (10 April)]. *Köznevelés – Minisztériumi rendeletek, közlemények*, *3*(13), 89–93.

movement and History of the Party in 1949; Dialectical-Historical materialism was also taught at this time.[18] In 1950, the Central Department of Marxism-Leninism was established at Eötvös Loránd University (ELTE) to organise the teaching of Marxism in higher education, catering to 30.000 students by 1951 (Borsodi & Tüskés, 2010, p. 203; Németh & Biró, 2016, pp. 53–56). As meeting the demand for university lecturers was among their short-term goals, the PC decided to organise a course solely dedicated to Marxism-Leninism at ELTE from 1952.[19] In the teacher training programmes, Marxism-Leninism (Philosophy or Political economy) was included between 1958 and 1960, while Philosophy and Teaching methods were part of the state examination, along with Pedagogy and thesis defence, between 1961 and 1968. From 1969, these were combined with subjects related to the specialisation programmes (Ladányi, 1999).

The status of education sciences in universities

According to contemporary studies on the relationship between pedagogy and educational sciences, the demands on pedagogy have notably increased (Faludi & Nagy, 1964, p. 14). The former was well-regarded as a science, while the latter was seen as a nascent discipline plagued with 'uncertain terminology' and 'taxonomic problems' contributing to its complexity. Progress was seen in the way that the field opened up to the scientific community, albeit with sufficient support. Professional opinions at the time highlighted the need for independent research institutes, believing that the main task of higher education was to teach, with research being a secondary function. The choice of topics, even in teacher training colleges, was primarily aligned with disciplinary areas rather than pedagogical content. It was noted that between 1950 and 1954, educational sciences lacked a dedicated research institute (Faludi & Nagy, 1964, pp. 14–15). During the 1950s, the Pedagogical Standing Committee of the HAS paved the way for the development of the 'new, socialist' educational sciences. Following the abolition of the National Institute of Educational Sciences, it served as the professional coordinator until the reestablishment of the institutional background. However, rather than merely overseeing university education departments, it also influenced the disciplinary discourse and education policy at the behest of the Party (Németh & Biró, 2016, p. 57).

18 NAH F. 276, u. 53/76. 5. Report about the session of the Political Committee of the Hungarian Working People's Party (MDP). Budapest, May 31, 1951.

19 NAH F. 276, u. 53/76. 9. Report about the session of the PC of the MDP. Budapest, May 31, 1951.

In the early years of this period, some experts recognised the need for research and the promotion of scientific careers in universities. However, they prioritised the training of 'socialist educators', including primary and secondary school teachers, as a major task (Jausz, 1959, pp. 691–692). Later, it was considered an 'honorary task' to conduct disciplinary research and integrate its results into the training pedagogues' curriculum. In the development of teacher training for secondary education, the relevant departments in the fields of educational sciences and psychology should have been given a greater role, but this required presenting further scientific achievements (Kardos, 1975).

Organisation of the Political Academy (PA)

The Party College of the Hungarian Working People's Party (*Magyar Dolgozók Pártja*, hereafter MDP) operated between 1949 and 1956. It was intended as an institution for 'the highest level of political cadres' training' (Ruzsa & Szabó, 2024), focusing on educating the political nomenclature rather than elevating a new social elite (Huszár, 2005). After the 1956 Revolution, the MSZMP critiqued the party schools as 'old, exaggerated, bureaucratic' relics of the Rákosi-era; their reorganisation began in December 1956 and involved former lecturers.[20]

From 1959, the Party College of the MSZMP worked on 'strengthening communist characteristics' by teaching theoretical and practical ideology.[21] With the gradual introduction of the major economic reform between 1964 and 1967, Sociology and Psychology (as well as Management Studies, Pedagogy, Rhetoric, and Aesthetics later on) were built into the curriculum to develop leadership skills. The institution (later renamed the PA) mandated that its college degree be recognised as equivalent to a state diploma when applying for various leading positions.[22] In 1968, its mission was redefined to provide ideological training for leaders of the CC, the lower-level party apparatus, state offices, and economic sectors.

After 1969, students with a PA degree were exempt from the rigorous examination required for the Marxism-Leninism minor subject.[23] Those who completed the pedagogical course were qualified to teach ideological subjects in Party

20 NAH F. 288, u. 5/11. 179–181. Report about the session of the PC. Budapest, January 14, 1957.

21 NAH F. 288, u. 5/97–98. 37., 555–559. Report about the session of the PC. Budapest, October 7, 1958.; NAH F. 288, u. 5/269. 241–245. Report about the session of the PC. Budapest, July 26, 1962.

22 NAH F. 288, u. 5/424. 389–392. Report about the session of the PC. Budapest, May 9, 1967.

23 146/1969. (VI. 20.) MM számú utasítás az egyetemi doktori címről.

schools, state colleges, and universities.[24] However, it was not until 1973 that the Department of Pedagogy at the PA was formally organised (Vörös, 1974, p. 153).[25] Afterwards, the PA was authorised to award the title 'Doctor of Political Sciences'; later, the CC recognised the defence of doctoral dissertations as a method of further training.[26] In the 1980s, the Party leadership sought to rationalise teaching and scientific work in its own institutions, encouraging cooperation with the HAS and university departments in order to enhance the quality of Marxist ideological training.[27]

At the end of the Kádár-era, the MSZMP tried to prepare for a multi-party system. Plans were made to replace the PA with the 'Institute of Political Theory' from 1990, with the government taking over the education of political sciences while ensuring the employment of teachers and the completion of students' courses. The PA was dissolved on December 31, 1989, with some students continuing their studies at the ELTE Institute of Sociology and others in the Political Theory programme established in 1994 (Kiss et al., 1999, p. 213).[28]

The separation of educational research from universities

National Institute of Educational Sciences (NIES)

The National Council for Public Education (NCPE) was founded in 1945 within the Ministry to rebuild public education, thereby ensuring that the results of science and experience were transferred to institutions, curricula, textbooks, and educational procedures (Kiss, 1957).[29] In 1947–48, the influence of the communist

24 NAH F. 288, u. 5/443. 113–115. Report about the session of the PC. Budapest, January 9, 1968.

25 The staff members of the Department were László Zrinszky (1973–1990), college professor, head of department in the National Institute of Pedagogy (NIP) and Katalin Nagy (1978–1988), candidate of education sciences, former researcher of the NIP (from 1978 both of them were associate professors at the PA).

26 158/1973. (VIII. 17.) MM számú utasítás a politikai tudományokban szerezhető egyetemi doktori címről; NAH F. 288, u. 5/746. 104. Report about the session of the PC. Budapest, May 16, 1978.

27 NAH F. 288, u. 5/972. 245–249. Report about the session of the PC. Budapest, July 1, 1986.

28 NAH F. 288, u. 59/3. 8–9., 51–53. Report about the session of the Leading Board of the MSZMP. Budapest, July 17, 1989.

29 1140/1945 (IV. 19.) ME számú rendelet az Országos Köznevelési Tanács felállítása tárgyában. The fragmentation of the research capacities related to education sciences can be followed in Table 2.

party grew through the centralisation of public education and the introduction of additional ideological materials. By 1948, plans were underway to establish an institution to support the Ministry; hence, the NIES replaced the NCPE in preparing legislative documents and advising on general issues in public education.[30] In an early draft indicated elements of a 'progressive' change in the 'traditional conservative' Hungarian educational sciences. Although the focus was mainly on Soviet research, scientists were expected to be able to politicise their work, although this did not mean that academic norms were solely politically derived (Deák, 1998, pp. 101–102; Knausz, 1986, p. 1090).

In 1950, the CC criticised the Ministry for the poor performance of primary schools and the failure of secondary school reform. 'Hostile activity' was identified within the institute and the NIES was labelled as 'a propagator of bourgeois educational sciences', leading to its dissolution by the Council of Ministers (CM) (Kardos, 2003, pp. 74–75; Knausz, 1986, p. 1100).[31]

Teachers' Central In-service Training Institute (TCITI)

Between 1948 and 1952, a transformation process in public education took place through legislation (Pukánszky, 1997). A central issue of this reform concerned the situation of teachers who had received their degrees before 1945, who had to adapt to the new 'Soviet-type' education system (Mann, 2002). In 1952, the TCITI, modelled after similar institutes in Moscow and Leningrad, was established within the Ministry as a college-like institute organised into departments. It was tasked with carrying out the further training of principals, school staff, and public education administrators.[32] While departments were mainly focused on specific subjects, there were also departments of Pedagogy, Primary Education, and Marxism-Leninism. Its staff formed expert committees with consultants from the Ministry, the Scientific Institute of Pedagogy, and the Textbook Publishing Company. At the departmental level, meetings were attended by the Party and trade union secretaries. According to the recollections, during this period many

30 11.160/1948 (X. 31.) Korm. számú rendelet az Országos Köznevelési Tanács működésének ideiglenes szüneteltetéséről.; 11.150/1948 (X. 31.) Korm. számú rendelet az Országos Neveléstudományi Intézet létesítése tárgyában.

31 122/1950 (IV. 29.) MT számú rendelet az Országos Neveléstudományi Intézet megszüntetése tárgyában.

32 1020/1952. (VII. 6.) MT számú határozat a Központi Pedagógus Továbbképző Intézet létesítéséről.

staff members were frequently contacted by the leading political forums (Kontra, 1972, p. 16).

In 1957, the primary objective of in-service training was to consolidate the Marxist-Leninist worldview among teachers. Following structural changes, the TCITI was abolished in 1962 (Kontra, 1972, p. 17).

Scientific Institute of Pedagogy (SIP)

After the dissolution of the NIES, pedagogy remained without a dedicated research institute until 1954, when the SIP was established. The move came at the suggestion of the CC, and coincided with the political turnaround of 1953.[33] The SIP set up a Department of Educational Theory and a Department of Educational History, alongside a separate Teacher Training Research Group. For many years, research in the field of subject pedagogy was dominated by the TCITI due to capacity issues. The main responsibilities of the SIP included the scientific processing of socialist education, the exploration of 'progressive pedagogical traditions', and examining the applicability of Soviet pedagogy. It also provided support in drafting various educational documents (such as the curricula of 1956–58 or the Law on Public Education of 1961). The staff maintained regular contact with the Ministry's school departments, taking part in meetings and reviewing the various materials, but publishing only from 1957 (Faludi & Szakra, 1958, pp. 536–538; Knausz, 1997; Simon, 1972, pp. 23–24).

National Institute of Pedagogy (NIP)

The NIP was founded in 1962 by merging the TCITI and the SIP.[34] It was tasked with writing curricula, educational programmes, organising study competitions, administering matura exams, and conducting research in the field of education sciences, and was also responsible for further training and supervision. It operated on a departmental basis, covering the various subjects and specific areas of education. Principles were generally governed by the ideology of Marxism-Leninism and the Party resolutions on educational policy; within this theoretical framework, the staff enjoyed a relatively high degree of freedom (Kardos, 1997). The NIP was dissolved on October 1, 1990 without a successor.[35]

---

33 2113/39/1954. MT számú határozat a Pedagógiai Tudományos Intézet létesítéséről.

34 1021/1962. (VIII. 12.) Korm. számú határozat az Országos Pedagógiai Intézet létesítéséről.

35 1/1990. (X. 1.) MKM számú utasítás az Országos Pedagógiai Intézet és a Nemzetközi Kulturális Intézet megszüntetéséről.

Higher Education Pedagogical Research Centre (PRC)

The PRC was established in 1967 by the Ministry through the division of the Higher Education Pedagogical Research Group of ELTE, which had existed since 1963. This new entity was created to provide scientific research results that would inform decisions on higher education.[36] It worked to expand both the theory and practice of pedagogy in Hungarian higher education (Völgyessy, 1997).

The role of the PRC was twofold: it coordinated general research activities in higher education and conducted educational science research programs. Their focus was on advertising for proposals and editing publications on a wide range of higher education issues, including studies on university admissions, the integration of recent graduates, didactics, institutional history, and comparative research. Initially, its publishing activity was mainly aimed at ensuring access to foreign literature in Hungary; however, a larger percentage of works by Hungarian authors also appeared over time (Jáki, 1971, 1982). Despite these efforts, the effectiveness of the PRC has been criticised from various angles (Vita, 1972, p. 20).

Due to the absence of a state authority to supervise research at universities, the Ministry set up the Scientific Council in 1974 to coordinate, monitor, and prepare proposals for the work of various institutes. The head of the PRC's Scientific Organisation Group also served as the Council secretary, handling administrative tasks (Tájékoztató a Művelődésügyi Minisztérium kutatásirányítási és kutatásszervezési modelljéről, 1974).[37]

Pedagogical Research Group of the Hungarian Academy of Sciences (PRG)

The governing board of the HAS decided on the establishment of the PRG in 1971, which was formalised by the Secretary-General of the HAS in 1972.[38] Founded to contribute to the development of educational science as well as youth and education policy, the PRG aimed to examine the contents and structure of education, the theoretical and methodological problems of research, and the study of youth movements. As the first academic research institute in education, its first years (1972–1975) were characterised by the dual tasks of conducting research at

36 122/1967. (VIII. 15.) MM számú utasítás a Felsőoktatási Pedagógiai Kutatóközpont szervezéséről.

37 109/1974. (IV. 1.) MM számú utasítás a Tudományos Tanács létesítéséről.

38 75/1971. számú MTA Elnökségi határozat a Pedagógiai Kutató Csoport megszervezéséről; 4/1972. 4/1972. MTA–F (A. K. 5.) számú MTA főtitkári utasítás a Pedagógiai Kutató Csoport létesítéséről.

an academic level and offering pragmatic results for the improvement of public education. The PRG was assigned with addressing the two sub-themes of the National Research Guidelines. Its operative principles and scientific concept were developed on the basis of the CC decision in 1972, aligning with the CM's science policy. Its focus included aspects of cadre recruitment and training, personnel qualifications, international cooperation, organising events and publications, as well as defining research objectives and performance evaluations.[39] The PRG was in charge of managing international relations, primarily with socialist countries, and collaborated with scientific institutes and university pedagogical departments in Hungary.[40] It played a coordinating role in the university pedagogical research departments and in the sub-centres founded at universities and colleges in 1973, which played an integral role in the implementation of institutional scientific programmes. As such, the PRG exercised significant administrative and organisational responsibilities in educational research.[41]

The scientific units of the PRG were the departments and the working groups with specific main tasks.[42] The internal training courses were professionally oriented, focusing on the development of awareness and insight into educational policy in cooperation with the Party and trade union organisations. Within this framework, 'suitable' researchers were given the opportunity to obtain an academic degree, while those without such status received targeted trained to carry out specific tasks. Research fellows prepared their doctoral theses in accordance with the overarching research plan. Another approach was ideological training, organised in collaboration with Party organisations and based on five-year political education plans. These measures aimed to enhance ideological-based academic preparation and to follow national and international achievements.[43] This helped facilitate the formation of working relations with 'friendly countries'

39 10.011/60/75 [Sine nomine] (Sine anno): Az MTA Pedagógiai Kutató Csoport beszámoló jelentése az 1972–1975. évi kutató tevékenységéről és működéséről. [Budapest]. p. 4. AHAS L V. Box 241, dossier 7.

40 PRG: Beszámoló az 1976–1980. évi kutatásokról. Budapest, December 31, 1980. 5. AHAS L XII. 705. Box 53., dossier 2.; PRG: „B" Működési Szabályzat, December 31, 1977. 2–4. AHAS L XII. 705. Box 55., dossier 6.

41 PRG: Szervezeti Szabályzat. Budapest, June 7, 1977. 3–6. AHAS L XII. 705. Box 55, dossier 6.; PRG: Beszámoló jelentés az 1972–1975. évi kutató tevékenységről és működésről. Budapest, December 31, 1980. 4. AHAS L XII. 705. Box 53., dossier 2.

42 PRG: Beszámoló jelentés az 1972–1975. évi kutató tevékenységről és működésről. Budapest, December 31, 1980. 4. AHAS L XII. 705. Box 53., dossier 2.

43 PRG: Középtávú Kutatási terv, 1976–1980. 38–40. AHAS L III. Box 227, dossier 2.

during the period of the first medium-term plan and expanded cooperation with Western countries and organisations during the second medium-term plan.

Due to the nature of educational scientific work, professional-ideological issues were regularly on the agenda at the PRG. Research into values, considered to be society-specific and moral-ideological, was a viewed as a priority. For the medium-term planning period of 1975–1980, the PRG defined two main research directions: the development of the state school system and the advancement of Marxist educational science.[44]

Institute for Educational Research (IER)

The IER was formed by the merger of the PRC and PRG under the Ministry in 1981.[45] Breaking with the tradition of its predecessors, the IER abandoned its pedagogical approach and became a social science think tank, conducting research on education policy (Lukács, 2001). The institute studied the socialisation processes of pupils, and initiated as well as managed experiments aimed at improving the educational system. This work was done in collaboration with research centres with a focus on school systems and included the performance of research tasks assigned by the Ministry. The IER also analysed the interactions between economic and social change and the education system in order to inform education policy decisions.

The IER conducted both basic and applied research addressing a wide range of topics, including the structure, policies, financing, development, history, and social aspects of primary, secondary, and higher education institutions as well as vocational training systems. These were examined at national, regional, local, and institutional levels. The results from these studies have been published in various forms (Imre, 1997). The IER was disbanded in 2004.[46]

National Education Technology Centre (NETC)

In response to the need for modernisation, the government envisioned a solution that established a national network based on existing foundations. To organise and manage this network, the NETC was established, supported financially and professionally by the UNESCO Development Programme, (Nagy, 1980; Nádasi, 2013).[47]

---

44 PRG: Középtávú Kutatási terv 1976–1980. 3. AHAS L XII. 705. Box 53., dossier 2.; PRG: Kutatási tervvázlat az 1981–1985-ös évekre. AHAS L III. Box 227, dossier 1.

45 105/1981 (III. 9.) MM számú utasítás az Oktatáskutató Intézet létesítéséről.

46 39/2003 (XII. 29.) OM számú rendelet az Oktatáskutató Intézet megszüntetéséről.

47 110/1973 (III. 1.) MM számú utasítás az Országos Oktatástechnikai Központ létesítéséről.

The main tasks of the NCET included research into educational technology, the coordination of information distribution in the country, the development and production of teaching tools, the training of educational technologists, and the provision of training for students and teachers. It also played an important role in experimenting with information media for public and higher education institutions and managing their publication. Among its notable achievements were School Television, educational films, the establishment of a closed-circuit television network, and the development of programmed education. Its staff also organised conferences, participated in international projects, and, in collaboration with educational technologists from regional educational institutions, took part in training courses abroad (Nádasi, 1980, 1997). The NETC continued to work as a company from 1991, and its successor still exists today.

Table 2: Dedicated research institutions for education sciences research activities (own editing)

Name of the institution (in English and in Hungarian)	Period of operation
National Institute of Educational Sciences (NIES) Országos Neveléstudományi Intézet	1948–1950
Teachers' Central In-service Training Institute (TCITI) Központi Pedagógus Továbbképző Intézet	1952–1962
Scientific Institute of Pedagogy (SIP) Pedagógiai Tudományos Intézet	1954–1962
National Institute of Pedagogy (NIP) Országos Pedagógiai Intézet	1962–1990
Higher Education Pedagogical Research Centre (PRC) Felsőoktatási Pedagógiai Kutatóközpont	(1963–) 1967–1981
Pedagogical Research Group of the Hungarian Academy of Sciences (PRG) Magyar Tudományos Akadémia Pedagógiai Kutatócsoportja	(1971) 1972–1981
Institute for Educational Research (IER) Oktatáskutató Intézet	1981–2004
National Education Technology Centre (NETC) Országos Oktatástechnikai Központ	1973– (1991)

Cooperation between research institutions in the long-term development plan for public education

The directives from the 10th Party Congress in 1970, along with the 1972 resolutions of the CC on the status of public education and the tasks required for its development, underscored the socio-political recognition that the 'complete construction' of socialism required further modernisation of public education. With this in mind, the national long-term scientific research plan was amended in 1973 to include pedagogical research aimed at improving public education by 1990.[48]

The review of the research plans showed that while the long-term development of the public education system was driven by socio-economic-technical developments, the system also expected to integrate with 'Marxist education science'. According to the Party, this integration fell short of expectations and its 'research base was unsatisfactory'. According to their criticisms, the research carried out in the research centres lacked a well-constructed plan, was uncoordinated, and in some cases was limited in scope. Furthermore, pedagogical sciences were only loosely linked with related co-disciplines and their institutions. The divergent development processes of research and teaching capacities were identified as a historical reason for these issues (A köznevelés fejlesztését szolgáló pedagógiai kutatások terve (1973–1990), 1974, p. 5). In order to improve, a better defined division of labour and the redefinition of institutional profiles were deemed necessary.

The Minister was responsible for defining the main research direction, while the CM was tasked with choosing research topics. The guidelines of the Party resolution on education policy were applied, stipulating the integration of short- and long-term tasks. The research tasks were divided into four major subtasks, each divided into smaller thematic groups. Each subtask was assigned to a base institution: the PRG dealt with basic systemic issues and long-term educational planning, focusing on the existential situation, communities, and political activities of young students. The NIP focused on modernising the content and methodology of public education and the further training of adults. The PRC organised efforts to study emerging issues in higher education, while the NIP managed the overall research coordination (Pósa, 1974, pp. 21–22; A köznevelés fejlesztését szolgáló pedagógiai kutatások terve (1973–1990), 1974, pp. 7–16).

Summary

This paper investigated changes in the institutional settings of education sciences in the decades after 1960. Additionally, it analysed the role of Party initiatives in shaping the institutional system. Throughout the investigation, a substantial

48 1035/1973 (VI. 19.) MT számú határozat az országos távlati tudományos kutatási terv kiegészítéséről.

number of archival sources were processed. Their interpretation aligned with periodical focal points deemed vital for understanding the general political shifts in Hungary.

A notable finding of the research is that the MSZMP rapidly adopted changes in education policy from the Soviet Union, tailoring them to Hungarian peculiarities during their implementation to maintain the stability of the political system (Rainer, 2011b). The scientific policy principles emanated from the Scientific-Technological Revolution declared at the 22nd Congress of the CPSU as well as the declaration on advanced socialism at the 24th Congress of 1971 were quickly implemented in Hungary. These principles had impacts both on the institutional system and the inner operational mechanisms of each institution (Kalmár, 2014, p. 187; p. 241). Nevertheless, the 1st Act of 1985 emerged primarily from Hungarian domestic political processes aimed at preserving state and party dominance over the education system. Considering the permission granted by the act to initiate curricular reforms and engage in alternative educational approaches in schools, the historiography of education sciences connected the act to the reform initiatives of the Soviet system that began in the spring of 1985. This view is still prevalent, with the act regarded as the first step towards system change in the educational affairs of Hungary (Báthory, 2001). Aligning Hungarian science policy with shifts in Soviet politics led to dual outcomes in the case of education sciences.

On the one hand, the training of teaching professionals and education research professionals were separated from each other, leading to the emergence of a fragmented institutional background of education sciences, characterised by fluctuations between uniforming and diverging political initiatives in decision-making. These fragmented institutional settings were inherited by the Kádár regime and were partly to the result of the system of colleges established for training primary teachers for elementary schools after 1945 (Ladányi, 2008, pp. 76–77; Romsics, 2004, p. 462). Additionally, the higher education policy between 1949–1955 further contributed to this fragmentation by dismantling the Humboldt-type full-universities and transforming them into multiple institutions with narrow research and training profiles. Later on, the separation of research and training capacities was reinforced by the new role assigned to the HAS after 1949 (Garai, 2016). Essentially, the Kádár regime modified this inherited structure by further fragmenting the institutional background of education research capacities. This agenda continued across political regimes, aiming to eliminate not only the Neohumanistic idea of the unity of research and teaching, crucial in the institutionalisation of modern education capacities, but also its institutional background (Horlacher, 2016, pp. 61–62).

On the other hand, implementing the shifts in Soviet scientific education policies led to new methods of scrutiny which were unprecedented in Hungarian history. Before 1955, the regime attempted to establish control over the academic sphere through administrative measures and by intervening in the methods of scientific disciplines, based on the methodological principles published by the Ministry of Higher Education (Garai, 2016, pp. 148–150). When the regime consolidated after 1956, the PA became a reference point in determining the ideological boundaries for scholars through the education of Marxism-Leninism. The PA and its graduates were authorised to oversee the implementation of the party policy across all levels of training, research programs, and activities of personnel in scientific institutions.

In this way, the PA was entrusted not only with training propagandists and researchers for upper party levels but also with exerting control over all scientific institutions, using new methods. From 1985, it also undertook the task of ideological development from a scientific point of view by merging political science methodology and Marxism-Leninism as a quasi-scientific discipline. This approach was meant to assist the party in reflecting on the development of its ideological course (Kalmár, 2014, p. 491). This intention emerged even before 1985, as indicated by the organisational structure of the PA, which followed university traditions and incorporated several scientific disciplines, including education sciences, into the training of propagandists and lecturers of Marxism-Leninism. The use of scientific principles in education was intended to enable party propagators to reflect on and interpret ideology from a scientific point of view. This anticipation also resulted in reform initiatives in the field of education sciences, which still adhered to party ideology despite also embracing Western ideas which were compatible with Socialism. These new reform initiatives developed in the institutions of education sciences played a crucial role in the education system changes of 1990 (Németh & Biró, 2016, p. 110).

Since 1989–1990, the fragmented institutional landscape of education sciences in Hungary have transformed significantly due to political and financial factors. Development perspectives of education sciences after 1990 have been shaped not only by the institutional background but also by the separation of research capacities and the training of scholars. Despite these changes, the discipline's focus on school and youth pedagogy,[49] a legacy from before the regime change, has remained intact. However, the divergent approaches emanating from the

49 PRG: Beszámoló az 1976–1980. évi kutatásokról. Budapest, December 31, 1980. AHAS XII. 705. Box 53., dossier 2.

fragmented institutional system are still present, resulting in parallel research activities that rarely intersect. These research activities can generally be categorised into two types according to their nature: applied investigations, which aim to improve the quality of education and thus align with social expectations, and theoretical research, which explores the fundamental questions of European and Hungarian education.

Indirectly, this research not only uncovered changes in the institutional settings of education sciences after 1960, including personal and political shifts, but also helped to provide a better understanding of the current dynamics determining the operation of the discipline today, an inevitable outcome of any historical research activity.

Bibliography

Primary sources

I. Almanacs

Az Eötvös Loránd Tudományegyetem értesítői. (1959/1960–1988/1989). [Annual Reports of the Eötvös Loránd University. (1959/1960-1988/1989)]. https://edit.elte.hu/xmlui/handle/10831/60/browse?rpp=20&sort_by=1&type=title&offset=60&etal=-1&order=ASC

Ketskeméty, I., Szentirmai, L., Csákány, B., Maróti, E., & Balogh, E. (Eds.). (1996). *Szegedi Egyetemi Almanach 1921–1995*. Hungaria. http://univ.bibl.u-szeged.hu/17976/1/egyetemi_almanach_1921_1995_1.pdf

Lengvári, I., & Polyák, P. (2017). *Pécsi Egyetemi Almanach 1367–1999*. https://almanach.pte.hu/impresszum

II. Archival sources

Magyar Nemzeti Levéltár Országos Levéltár [National Archives of Hungary, National Archive] (MNL OL)

Magyar Szocialista Munkáspárt Politikai Bizottságának ülései [Sessions of the Political Committee of the Hungarian Socialist Workers' Party] (MSZMP PB)

Fonds 288, unit 5/356. Session of March 16, 1965.

Fonds 288, unit 5/1079. Session of October 3, 1989.

Magyar Szocialista Munkáspárt Központi Bizottságának ülései [Sessions of the Central Committee of the Hungarian Socialist Workers' Party] (MSZMP KB)

Fonds 288, unit 4/73–74. 11–13 March 1965.

Fonds 288, unit 4/264/265. 23–24 June 1989.

Magyar Szocialista Munkáspárt Titkárságának ülései [Sessions of the Secretary of the Hungarian Socialist Workers' Party] (MSZMP Titkárság)

Fonds 288, unit 7/152. January 11, 1963.

Fonds 288, unit 7/805. May 9, 1989.

Magyar Tudományos Akadémia Levéltára (MTA L) [Archives of the Hungarian Academy of Sciences]

Fonds III: Az MTA Hivatala [Bureau of the Hungarian Academy of Sciences]. MTA Társadalomtudományi Főosztály iratai, 1970–1990 [Documents of the Social Sciences Department of the Hungarian Academy of Sciences].

Box 227. Beszámolók, tervek. [Reports, proposals].

Fonds V: Az MTA Testülete [Scientific Boards of the Hungarian Academy of Sciences]. 102. Magyar Tudományos Akadémia II. Filozófiai- és Történettudományok Osztályának iratai 1950–2006 [102 Documents of the II. Philosophical and Historical Department of the Hungarian Academy of Sciences].

Box 241. Kutatási beszámolók az 1972–1975-ös tervperiódusról. [Scientific Reports on the period of 1972–1975]

Fonds XII. 705: Pedagógiai Kutatócsoport [Research Group for Pedagogy]

Box 53. Tudományos beszámolók, 1980 [Scientific Reports, 1980].

Box 55. Tudományos beszámolók, 1981 [Scientific Reports, 1981].

Secondary sources

A köznevelés fejlesztését szolgáló pedagógiai kutatások terve (1973–1990). (1974). *Magyar Pedagógia*, *74*(1), 3–16.

Báthory, Z. (2000). A maratoni reform. 1. rész. *Iskolakultúra*, *10*(1), 45–60. https://www.iskolakultura.hu/index.php/iskolakultura/article/view/19348/19138

Báthory, Z. (2001). *Maratoni reform*. Ökonet.

Borsodi, Cs., & Tüskés, A. (2010). *Az Eötvös Loránd Tudományegyetem Bölcsészettudományi Karának története képekben 1635–2010*. Eötvös Loránd Tudományegyetem Bölcsészettudományi Kar. http://real.mtak.hu/7590/1/1.1.3.pdf

Coffey, A. (2014). Analysing Documents. In U. Flick (Ed.), *The SAGE Handbook of Qualitative Data Analysis* (pp. 367–379). SAGE Publications.

Darvai, T. (2021). Makarenko-értelmezések Magyarországon a hosszú 1950-es években. *Iskolakultúra*, *31*(5), 27–40. https://doi.org/10.14232/ISKKULT.2021.05.27

Deák, F. (1998). Az új nevelés kérdései. *Új Pedagógiai Szemle*, *48*(11), 101–104.

Faludi, Sz., & Nagy, L. (1964). A magyar neveléstudomány helyzete és feladatai. *Magyar Tudomány, 71*(1), 14–20. http://real-j.mtak.hu/164/1/MATUD_1964.pdf

Faludi, Sz., & Szarka, J. (1958). A Pedagógiai Tudományos Intézet (PTI) munkájáról. In Á. Kiss (Ed.), *Tanulmányok a neveléstudomány köréből 1958* (pp. 529–538). Akadémiai Kiadó. https://real-j.mtak.hu/5556/1/TanulmanyokNevelestudomanyKorebol_1958.pdf

Garai, I. (2016). A magyar felsőoktatás strukturális átalakítási és államosítási kísérletei az 1949–1953 közötti időszakban. In A. Németh, I. Garai, & Z. A. Szabó (Eds.), *Neveléstudomány és pedagógiai kommunikáció a szocializmus időszakában* (pp. 119–160). Gondolat Kiadó. http://real.mtak.hu/39151/1/PTE_Nemeth_javitott.pdf

Golnhofer, E. (2004). Pedagógusok változó politikai viszonyok között. *Iskolakultúra, 14*(10), 75–83. http://real.mtak.hu/60296/1/EPA00011_iskolakultura_2004_10_075-083.pdf

Golnhofer, E., & Szabolcs, É. (2020). A Szocialista Nevelés Könyvtára 1950–1957. Politikai termék vagy tudományos produktum? In I. Garai, K. Kempf, & B. Vincze (Eds.), *Mestermunka: A neveléstudomány aktuális diskurzusai* (pp. 160–173). L'Harmattan.

Hopfner, J., Németh, A., & Szabolcs, É. (Eds.). (2009). *Kindheit. Schule-Erziehungswissenschaft in Mitteleuropa 1948–2008*. Peter Lang.

Horlacher, R. (2016). *The Educated Subject and the German Concept of Bildung. A Comparative Cultural History*. Roudledge.

Horn, K.-P. (2003). *Erziehungswissenschaft in Deutschland im 20. Jahrhundert*. Klinkhardt.

Horváth, A. (2016). A szovjet típusú diktatúra oktatáspolitikája Magyarországon. *Polgári Szemle, 12*(1–3), 94–114. https://polgariszemle.hu/images/content/pdf/psz_2016._1-3.szam_8.pdf

Huszár, T. (2005). Az elittől a nómenklatúráig: Az intézményesített káderpolitika kialakulása és néhány jellemzője Magyarországon (1945–1989). *Szociológiai Szemle, 15*(3), 8–69. https://szociologia.hu/dynamic/0503huszar.pdf

Imre, A. (1997). Oktatáskutató Intézet. In Z. Báthory, & I. Falus (Eds.), *Pedagógiai Lexikon* (Vol. 3, pp. 32–33). Keraban Könyvkiadó.

Jáki, L. (1971). Eredmények és gondok. A Felsőoktatási Pedagógiai Kutatóközpont munkája. *Felsőoktatási Szemle, 20*(11), 647–650.

Jáki, L. (1982). A Felsőoktatási Pedagógiai Kutatóközpont kiadványairól. *Magyar Pedagógia, 82*(3), 285–286. http://real-j.mtak.hu/4796/1/MagyarPedagogia_1982.pdf

Jausz, B. (1959). A tudományegyetemeken alakított szakmódszertani munkaközösségek feladatai. *Felsőoktatási Szemle, 8*(11), 691–696.

Kardos, J. (1975). A tudományegyetemek és a tanárképző intézmények három évtizedes fejlődése. *Felsőoktatási Szemle, 24*(4), 203–208.

Kardos, J. (1997). Országos Pedagógiai Intézet. In Báthory, Z., & Falus, I. (Eds.), *Pedagógiai Lexikon* (Vol. 3, pp. 77–78). Keraban Könyvkiadó.

Kardos, J. (2003). Fordulat a magyar iskolák életében: A Rákosi-időszak oktatáspolitikája. *Iskolakultúra, 13*(6–7), 73–80. https://epa.oszk.hu/00000/00011/00072/pdf/iskolakultura_EPA00011_2003_06_07_073-080.pdf

Kalmár, M. (1998). *Ennivaló és hozomány: A kora kádárizmus ideológiája.* Magvető Kiadó.

Kalmár, M. (2014). *Történelmi galaxisok vonzásában: Magyarország és a szovjetrendszer 1945–1990.* Osiris Kiadó.

Kelemen, E. (2003). Oktatáspolitikai irányváltozások Magyarországon a 20. század második felében (1945–1990). *Új Pedagógiai Szemle, 53*(9), 25–32.

Kéri, K. (2001). *Bevezetés a neveléstörténeti kutatások módszertanába.* Műszaki Könyvkiadó.

Kiss, Á. (1957). Hogyan működött az Országos Köznevelési Tanács? *Köznevelés, 13*(1), 11–12.

Kiss, J. M., Szögi, L., & Varga, J. (1999). *Az Eötvös Loránd Tudományegyetem Levéltára, repertórium 1635–1990* (Vol. 2). Eötvös Loránd Tudományegyetem Levéltára. https://library.hungaricana.hu/hu/view/ELTE_Tort_20/

Knausz, I. (1986). A magyar "pedológia" pere - 1948–1950. *Pedagógiai Szemle, 36*(11), 1087–1102.

Knausz, I. (1997). Pedagógiai Tudományos Intézet. In Z. Báthory, & I. Falus (Eds.), *Pedagógiai Lexikon* (Vol. 3, p. 159). Keraban Könyvkiadó.

Kontra, Gy. (1972). Központi Pedagógus Továbbképző Intézet. In I. Bori (Ed.), *Országos Pedagógiai Intézet 1962–1972* (pp. 10–22). Országos Pedagógiai Intézet.

Kudlacová, B., & Rajsky, A. (2019). *Education and "Pädagogik". Philosophical and Historical Reflections.* Peter Lang.

Ladányi, A. (1999). *A magyar felsőoktatás a 20. században.* Akadémiai Kiadó.

Ladányi, A. (2008). *A középiskolai tanárképzés története.* Új Mandátum Kiadó.

Lukács, P. (2001). Kutatás vagy politikaformálás? *Educatio, 10*(1), 94–102. https://epa.oszk.hu/01500/01551/00015/pdf/1106.pdf

Mann, M. (2002). *Budapest oktatásügye 1873–2000.* Ökonet.

Nádasi, A. (1980). Az oktatástechnológia hazai oktatásának fejlődése az Országos Oktatástechnikai Központ és bázishálózata tevékenységének tükrében (1973–1979). I. rész. *Audio-Vizuális Közlemények, 17*(2), 114–120.

Nádasi, A. (1997). Országos Oktatástechnikai Központ. In Z. Báthory, & I. Falus (Eds.), *Pedagógiai Lexikon* (Vol. 3, p. 77). Keraban Könyvkiadó.

Nádasi, A. (2013). *Oktatásfejlesztési és -technológiai kutatások*. Médiainformatikai Kiadványok.

Nagy, J. (1980). *The Hungarian experience of OOK: An instrument for the development of educational technology*. UNESCO.

Németh, A. (2015). Főbb tudományelméleti irányzatok, kutatási eredményeik és hatásuk nemzetközi és hazai neveléstudomány-tudománytörténeti kutatásokra. In A. Németh, Zs. H. Biró, & I. Garai (Eds.), *Neveléstudomány és tudományos elit a 20. század második felében* (pp. 9–81). Gondolat Kiadó. http://real.mtak.hu/35462/1/Nevelestudomany_törd_1.pdf

Németh, A., Biró, Zs. H., & Garai, I. (Eds.). (2015). *Neveléstudomány és tudományos elit a 20. század második felében*. Gondolat Kiadó. http://real.mtak.hu/35462/1/Nevelestudomany_törd_1.pdf

Németh, A., Biró, Zs. H. (2016). A magyar neveléstudomány diszciplína jellemzőinek és kognitív tartalmainak változásai a 20. század második felében. In A. Németh, I. Garai, & Z. A. Szabó (Eds.), *Neveléstudomány és pedagógiai kommunikáció a szocializmus időszakában* (pp. 53–56). Gondolat Kiadó. http://real.mtak.hu/39151/1/PTE_Nemeth_javitott.pdf

Németh, A., Garai, I., & Szabó, Z. A. (Eds.). (2016). *Neveléstudomány és pedagógiai kommunikáció a szocializmus időszakában*. Gondolat Kiadó. http://real.mtak.hu/39151/1/PTE_Nemeth_javitott.pdf

Orosz, I., & Barta, J. (Eds.). (2012). *A Debreceni Egyetem története 1912–2012*. Debreceni Egyetemi Kiadó. https://mek.oszk.hu/18400/18465/18465.pdf

Polónyi, I., & Kozma, T. (2020). A magyar felsőoktatás fejlődése a rendszerváltás után. *Magyar Tudomány, 181*(4), 502–512. http://doi.org/10.1556/2065.181.2020.4.8.

Pósa, Zs. (1974). A köznevelés fejlesztését szolgáló pedagógiai kutatásokról. *Pedagógiai Szemle, 24*(1), 19–27.

Pukánszky, B. (1997). Az 1945 utáni magyar iskoláztatás történetének vázlata. In B. Pukánszky, & A. Németh (Eds.), *Neveléstörténet* (pp. 575–584). Nemzeti Tankönyvkiadó.

Rainer M., J. (2011a). Magyarország a Szovjetunió árnyékában, 1944–1989. In J. Rainer M. (Ed.), *Bevezetés a Kádárizmusba* (pp. 13–38). L'Harmattan.

Rainer M., J. (2011b). Kádárizmus. In J. Rainer M. (Ed.), *Bevezetés a Kádárizmusba* (pp. 93–214). L'Harmattan.

Romsics, I. (2004). *Magyarország története a XX. században*. Osiris Kiadó.

Ruzsa, B., & Szabó, Z. A. (2024). The recruitment of Party College students of the Hungarian Working People's Party (1949–1956). In Z. A. Szabó, L. Somogyvári, I. Garai, & A. Németh (Eds.), *Evolving perspectives: The development of Hungarian educational science after 1945* (pp. 53–74). Peter Lang.

Simon, Gy. (1963). Neveléstörténeti kutatás levéltárakban. In Á. Kiss, S. Nagy, J. Szarka, & I. Szokolszky (Eds.), *Tanulmányok a neveléstudomány köréből 1962* (pp. 249–278). Akadémiai Kiadó. https://real-j.mtak.hu/5566/1/TanulmanyokNevelestudomanyKorebol_1962.pdf

Simon, Gy. (1972). Pedagógiai Tudományos Intézet. Előzmények és a PTI megszervezése. In I. Bori (Ed.), *Országos Pedagógiai Intézet 1962–1972* (pp. 23–24). Országos Pedagógiai Intézet.

Somogyvári, L. (2021). „Iskolareformok" a szocialista blokkon belül (1958–1965). In P. Maisch, Zs. Molnár-Kovács, & H. P. Szabó (Eds.), *Iskola a társadalmi térben és időben* (Vol. 8, pp. 36–43). Pécsi Tudományegyetem Bölcsészet- és Társadalomtudományi Kar „Oktatás és Társadalom" Neveléstudományi Doktori Iskola. https://btk.pte.hu/sites/btk.pte.hu/files/nevtudphd/Kiadványok/Iskola társadalmi térben és időban 8.pdf

Szabolcs, É. (Ed.). (2006). *Pedagógia és politika a XX. század második felében Magyarországon*. Eötvös József Könyvkiadó.

Szabolcs, É. (2011). Deduktív (Analitikus) jellegű kutatások. In I. Falus (Ed.), *Bevezetés a pedagógiai kutatás módszereibe* (pp. 84–94). Műszaki Könyvkiadó.

Tájékoztató a Művelődésügyi Minisztérium kutatásirányítási és kutatásszervezési modelljéről. (1974). *Akadémiai Közlöny*, *23*(1), 6–7. https://real-j.mtak.hu/8344/1/MTA_AkademiaiErtesito_1974_23.pdf

Vita. (1972). *A Politikai Főiskola Közleményei*, *2*(1), 19–23.

Völgyesy, P. (1997). Felsőoktatási Pedagógiai Kutató Központ. In Z. Báthory, & I. Falus (Eds.), *Pedagógiai Lexikon* (Vol. 3: p. 486). Keraban Könyvkiadó.

Vörös, B. (1974). A Politikai Főiskola oktatóinak és munkatársainak szakirodalmi munkássága II. *A Politikai Főiskola Közleményei*, *4*(2), 129–173.

Wernet, A. (2014). Hermeneutics and Objective Hermeneutics. In U. Flick (Eds.), *The SAGE Handbook of Qualitative Data Analysis* (pp. 234–246). SAGE Publications.

Bence Ruzsa,[1] Zoltán András Szabó[2]

The recruitment of students in the Party College of the Hungarian Working People's Party (1949–1956)[3]

Abstract: Following the Second World War, the Hungarian Communist Party (*Magyar Kommunista Párt*, hereafter MKP) strove to secure influence in all spheres of society, culminating in a complete takeover by the end of 1940s. This resulted in the establishment of a *system of nomenclature* which prevented the emergence of a new *elite*. According to Huszár (2002), the distinction between the terms of nomenclature and elite lies in that members of the ruling class ascend based on individual merits and accomplishments, whereas candidates for the nomenclature are appointed irrespective of these criteria by a governing body endowed with authoritative powers. The latter method is essential in a structure in which political positions have strategic value, such as in the centralised, dependency-based relations of the one-party system. The upper echelons of the elite are only accessible to a certain group of leaders, while the imposition of political principles and the removal of transparency in personnel policy (resulting from the control over functionaries by the ruling party) results in distortions in their recruitment and socialisation. In the new political system, the artificially centralised recruitment mechanism of the elite became one of the most tightly planned and controlled processes (Körösényi, 1998, pp. 41–47), serving as a crucial element in the preservation of the monopoly power of the Hungarian Working People's Party (*Magyar Dolgozók Pártja*, hereafter MDP).

Keywords: Rákosi-regime, nomenclature, cadre system, Marxism-Leninism, party education

---

1 Doctoral School of Education, ELTE Eötvös Loránd University, Budapest, Hungary, ruzsa.bence@ppk.elte.hu

2 Institute of Education, ELTE Eötvös Loránd University, Budapest, Hungary, szabo.zoltan.andras@ppk.elte.hu

3 This paper is a shortened and edited version of the research work that was submitted to the 36th National Conference of Scientific Students' Associations [Országos Tudományos Diákköri Konferencia] in 2023, where Bence Ruzsa won first prize in the 'Subsection of the History of Education and Pedagogy', and was also awarded the Pro Scientia Gold Medal.

Introduction

To date, there has been a lack of fundamental research on the history of the MDP's party education and school network between 1945 and 1956, including even micro-level, systematic studies of individual Party schools (Huhák, 2016, p. 84). One possible reason for this gap is that the papers written in this topic area are more focused on the development of public and higher education for the broader masses during the Rákosi-era.

The structuring of society under communist rule typically followed Soviet models, and were orchestrated by the Central Committee of the Communist Party of the Soviet Union (CPSU). Here, three main levels of specialised training for the Party and state apparatus can be identified: a network of seminars and courses organised by local party offices, 'party schools' and 'higher party schools' at the level of the upper administrative units, and the Academy of Social Sciences at the top of the hierarchy (Matthews, 2012, p. 184; Roucek, 1958, p. 99). From 1945, the MKP also established similar party schools in Hungary. These included three-four-week-long county schools on the lower level, six-week and three-month schools on the middle level, and five or six-month-long Central Party Schools (hereafter CPS) at the upper level that provided ideological education for certain groups of functionaries (MDP KV Oktatási Osztály, 1948). In this system, just as in the Soviet model, the same training methods were applied at each level, with the primary difference between them being the breadth of material to be acquired (Ispán, 2021; Roucek, 1958, p. 99).

After the end of communism in Hungary in 1989, researchers were motivated to explore the history of education in Hungary after 1945 without political and ideological influences (Golnhofer, 2004; Szabó et al., 2022). Despite these efforts, the *Pártfőiskola* [Party College, hereafter College] of the MDP has not yet been the subject of such an endeavour. The institution, similarly to the Higher Party Schools in the Soviet Union (Rutland, 1993, p. 190), considered itself, through its tasks and structure, to be part of 'higher education'.[4] Nevertheless, it was not integrated into the state school system and was positioned outside (or above) its structure (Németh & Biró, 2016, p. 40).

4 Until 1952, Party decrees related to the Party College did not use an exact term for the institution's classification within the educational hierarchy (i.e., whether it was considered a college, a university, or another type of school). Prior to this, these documents usually referred to the institution by its name or simply as a 'school'. However, in both the regulatory documents and in the Director's reports, there is language (e.g., 'academy', 'scientific excellence', 'undergraduate students', or 'departments') that suggests a 'college identity'. For a more detailed overview of this issue, see the sub-chapter '*Status and connection to ideological training in higher education*'.

This paper focuses on the institution that operated until the Revolution of 1956, at which point it was disbanded with the dissolution of the MDP, and reorganised from the end of the year. It also served as the predecessor of the *Politikai Főiskola* [Political Academy] of the Central Committee of the Hungarian Socialist Workers' Party (*Magyar Szocialista Munkáspárt*, hereafter MSZMP), that trained party functionaries during the Kádár-era.

Research questions

In the historical discourse on education policy after 1948 in Hungarian public and higher education, one of the defining elements is the ideology-based discriminatory category system implemented by the ruling Party. This provided advantages to certain social groups and partly ensured the replenishment of their leadership layers, thereby generating social inequalities. The criteria and operation of this system are already known through previous research (Ladányi, 1995; Sáska, 2021; Somogyvári, 2015). The questions of the present investigation aim to elucidate the process by which the leading party selected candidates for training in higher leadership positions within its own nomenclature system:

1. Which Party organs were involved in determining the student composition?
2. What was the connection between the initial change in the institution's organisational form and the enforcement of the training organisation goals of the party organs?
3. How did structural changes affect the admission process?
4. How were the criteria for the admission process formed?
5. What are the characteristics that distinguish the Party College as a higher education institution?

Sources

Several factors made it difficult to examine the topic at hand, including the identification of sources, comparability with other party schools, and embeddedness in the institutional network. The institution was not autonomous in the development of its organisation and training system nor in the execution of its admission procedures, and its operation was essentially influenced by the central party leadership. Therefore, archival documents generated during the decision-making process from these central bodies have been identified as primary sources (T. Varga, 1998).

These documents are connected with the MDP (M-KS Fonds 276) and are preserved in the National Archives of Hungary (NAH) (T. Varga, 2005). The materials are available via the archival service *AdatbázisokOnline*[5] [Databases Online], which provides information on organs such as the *Párt- és Tömegszervezetek Osztálya* [Department of Party and Mass Organisations, hereafter DPMO], the *Agitációs és Propaganda Osztály* [Agitation and Propaganda Department, hereafter APD], and until 1952 the *Káder Osztály* [Cadres' Department], which were responsible for managing and controlling the lower-level organs and institutions of the Party apparatus, including Party schools. They also collected and disseminated the candidate suggestions for cadres, operating under the authority of the *Központi Vezetőség* [Central Leadership, hereafter CL].

Personal data tables with suggestions were attached and submitted to the MDP's leading operational organs; during meetings of the *Politikai Bizottság*[6] [Political Committee, hereafter PC], the *Titkárság*[7] [Secretariat], and the *Szervező Bizottság*[8] [Organising Committee, hereafter OC], these lists were discussed and decisions were made regarding the classification of students transfers, and possible recalls at each level of party training. Among these documents, the earliest data table, a list of names, was dated to August 1951.

Methods

Information in the present study was extracted from primary sources partly through the use of prosopography: personal data were collected on a sheet (which has not been included here for reasons of scope). Prosopography can be applied in social science research and social history writing to study and address two important historical issues. The first pertains to problems rooted in political activities, and may involve, for example, the uncovering of underlying interests (social affiliation of groups or political mechanisms) that are assumed to be hidden by political rhetoric. The second one is related to the structure of society and internal mobility, entailing the analysis of the social roles of members of elite groups and those holding official positions, as well as the changes in these roles over time (Stones, 1971). As such, this approach systematically gathers all pertinent biographical information about individuals from a specific group based on their shared background and characteristics, organising this data into a structured table (Engel, 2002; Verboven et al., 2007). An examination of international terminology by Bara (2002) highlights the difference between prosopography and collective biography,

---

5 See the website here: https://adatbazisokonline.mnl.gov.hu/.

6 National Archives of Hungary (NAH) Fonds (F.) 276, unit (u.) 53.

7 NAH F. 276, u. 54.

8 NAH F. 276, u. 55.

terms which are often used interchangeably. In her analysis, she outlines the most important features that differentiate the two approaches (see Table 1).

Table 1: Comparison of collective biography and prosopography in social history writing based on the genre characteristics (adapted from Engel, 2002 and Bara, 2007)

	Characteristics in collective biographical works	**Characteristics in prosopographic works**
The subject of the research	a given person	a small or large group (focus on a given person is only relevant on the basis of group membership)
Tries to fully explore the subject's path of life	yes	no
The range of analysed data	more detailed and complete data collection	data is collected which is relevant to the research
Use of narratives	used	not used
Results	historical (descriptive) work	data sheet of personal information
Recognising preserved memories from the personal past	possible	not possible

In summary, it can be claimed that prosopography is suitable for systematically examining all members of a given (e.g., elite) group to identify and describe the common characteristics, such as properties and behaviours, that are valid for the whole group (Németh & Szabolcs, 2002). Broady (2002) considers the so-called 'French prosopography' developed by Pierre Bourdieu and his colleagues as a variant of this method. Its distinctiveness lies in its integration of the principles of Bourdieu's field theory with the general traits of prosopography. A central element of the approach is that all examined persons belong to a common field,[9] and the

9 According to Bourdieu (2005), it can be stated that symbolic capitals such as loyalty and recognition are accumulated by political groups during their battles, and they build an organisation capable of mobilising those who sympathize with them. This apparatus can rely on two elements of the organisational structure: on the one hand, in bureaucratic institutions of the party they can acquire positions (and thus privileges), on the other hand, in return for this they must be loyal to the party and accept the central decisions. The relationship will be based on the fact that the party as an institution takes care of those who show loyalty, because it knows that its activists depend on it to prevail, they cannot deny this without having to do the same to themselves.

data collection must be organised according to variables that allow for an analysis of their origins, education background, career, and position within the field.

According to Bara (2007), three main lines of inquiry must be addressed in order to perform the analysis. These include the examining the standards that were followed during the data collection, the criteria for participation in the data collection, and the structures that help to ensure transparency when presenting the data. Paksa (2013) recommends that the group to be investigated should be well determined and sufficiently large, and that preestablished and transparent criteria should be considered to avoid a shortage of data. Thanks to computer-aided data recording, unnecessary copying can be minimised, and the consistency of recorded data as well as the correction of errors can be promptly ensured (Mawdsley & Munck, 1996).

The process began with the identification of the data tables included in the proposals submitted by the departments of the CL. In the 1950s, these departments typically described candidates using the same set of personal data: name, year of birth, original profession, current workplace, and position at the time of nomination. The next step was to record data in a Microsoft Excel worksheet (Kontra, 2011) and lastly to delete the duplicate records.

To interpret the results obtained using prosopography, the context has to be established via historical source analysis. This is supported by the principle that fragments of the past can never be understood without examining the whole concept (Simon, 2000). Accordingly, research in the history of education can be particularly valuable, as it can draw attention to the significance of sensitivity in identifying historical facts and phenomena. Furthermore, it facilitates the recognition of connections and processes (through examples from pedagogical history) and can support the critical evaluation of past theoretical and practical mistakes in education (Kéri, 2001).

In-depth studies of institutional histories can also be included in the framework of educational history studies using a diachronic approach. The heuristic phase of the research involves identifying primary and secondary sources, determining their availability, and recording the data as they are processed.[10] The recorded data are then sorted into sub-groups according to themes (e.g., the content of the teaching, developments in staffing, and subject conditions) relevant to the period under study (Kéri, 2001).

10 This process typically involves extracting the content of the sources and recording verbatim quotations, with the possibility of associating one's own thoughts where appropriate. These materials can then be utilised in subsequent analyses to address the previously formulated questions.

External and internal source criticism is particularly important given that the specificities of the Rákosi-era led to considerable bias in the interpretations of these years found in written sources. This bias primarily stems from the authoritarianism inherent in the hierarchical structure of the MDP, in which conformity to higher party bodies played was a characteristic feature. A more realistic picture of the operational conditions can emerge when an event disrupts the rules of the system's framework (Huhák, 2016, p. 85). There are additional factors that contribute to the complexity of understanding the ideological system (and have shaped perspectives on educational sciences), such as the concept of political religion and the presence of quasi-sacred elements (e.g., the ideology of Marxism-Leninism or the 'unquestionable historical role' of Lenin). Such factors play a strong role in forming content associations in regard to secondary meanings (Somogyvári et al., 2021). These ideas were further developed in the hermeneutic phase of the research, which, in view of the complex social processes of the time, requires a detailed and thorough scientific orientation and a sense of reality (Kéri, 2001).

Results

Formation of the College

The presence of alternative institutions shaping a democratic elite posed a challenge that the communists were determined to address. One example was the Vasvári Pál Academy: the autonomous and value-based institution, similar to the National Association of People's Colleges with its innovative pedagogical initiatives, was dissolved in 1949 (Pukánszky & Németh, 1995, p. 577). These were replaced by a cadre training institution for the leading functionaries under the ruling Party, the Party College (Huszár, 2002).

In May 1949, amidst concerns about the inability of the lower party schools to guarantee the required level of preparation, a proposal was put forward to organise 'autumn Party schools' (later referred to as the two-year 'Communist Academy'). The lack of a specialised educational facilities for 'top cadres' was identified as a factor contributing to the low number of lecturers (e.g., heads, assistants, and seminar leaders) in the ideology departments of colleges and universities. To address this, it was suggested to establish three new schools within the CPS framework aimed at training various groups of functionaries. Among these was the Academy, which was planned to launch with 70–80 students in the autumn of 1949.[11]

11 NAH F. 276, unit 54/42. 36–38. Report about the session of the Secretariat. Budapest, May 7, 1949.

The two-year Party College was organised in the fall of 1949,[12] and was intended to have two main functions: on the one hand, it aimed to train 'well-qualified' propagandist cadres and instructors for the lower-level Party schools. On the other hand, it was tasked with producing teaching materials (including outlines and lecture texts) for teaching ideology in Party schools, state colleges, and universities. The inaugural academic year of the two-year Party College commenced on October 20, 1949,[13] and at the same time the one-year College also began operating in Budapest, on the site of the former CPS[14] (Huba & Szabó, 1998).

In 1950, it was proposed for the two institutions to be consolidated into a single building, thus improving the division of labour between teachers, standardising policies, and streamlining their organisation.[15] In the autumn of 1951, the colleges shared the same building, and were collectively renamed the 'Party College of the MDP'.

Table 2: Structure of the College between 1949 and 1956 (own editing)

Schooling form	Existence	Modification
one-year Party College	1949–1952	renamed in 1952 as 'one-year Party School'[16]
two-year Party College	1949–1954	training period increased to 3 years[17]
three-year Party College	1953–1956	dissolved in the autumn of 1956
correspondence course (based on the two-year College)	1953–1954	reorganised after the establishment of the three-year Party College[18]
correspondence course (based on the three-year College)	1954–1956	dissolved in the autumn of 1956

12 NAH F. 276, u. 53/37. 3–7. Report about the session of the PC. Budapest, October 6, 1949.

13 NAH F. 276, u. 53/37. 2. Report about the session of the PC. Budapest, October 6, 1949.

14 Budapest City Archives XXXV.95.a. 140. 189. Request of the one-year Party College. Budapest, October 14, 1949.

15 NAH F. 276, 54/98. 4. Report about the session of the PC. Budapest, May 3, 1950.

16 Due to the need to distinguish between one- and two-year courses because of their differing study time frames for study, it was decided that only the two-year course would be designated as the 'Party College' from 1952 (NAH F. 276, u. 54/202. 25. Report about the session of the Secretariat. Budapest, July 24, 1952.)

17 NAH F. 276, u. 54/206. 15. Report about the session of the Secretariat. Budapest, August 13, 1952.

18 NAH F. 276, u. 54/348. 79. Report about the session of the Secretariat. Budapest, December 9, 1954.

Schooling form	Existence	Modification
10-month correspondence course (further training of 'leading cadres')[19]	1955–1956	dismissal from the next academic year was decided in May 1956[20]
three-year aspirantura[21]	1955–1956	dissolved in the autumn of 1956
five-year correspondence course	1956	dissolved in the autumn of 1956

During the Revolution of 1956, a temporary emergency hospital operated in the building of the College until 9 November (Szakolczai, 2014, p. 113). The MSZMP, which came to power after the Revolution, reorganised the Party school system, criticising it as an 'old, exaggerated, bureaucratic' element of the MDP's activity.[22] By the end of 1956, the temporary Party schools for the transitional period were organised, and almost three years later the renewed two-year institution, the Party College of the Central Committee of the MSZMP, was set to begin its work (Ruzsa et al., 2024).[23]

The educational profile

After the first few months of operation, changes were required. Starting in the autumn of 1950, the two-year College transitioned from its previous 'lecturer-training' profile to a focus on training leading party functionaries (e.g., county secretaries, deputy heads of departments and sub-department heads, and Party school lecturers). Meanwhile, the one-year College trained political staff of the central Party apparatus, members of county committees, district Party secretaries, and central leaders of mass organisations.[24]

The continuous revisions of the Party school system were always aimed at ensuring that as many people as possible (particularly party members) received some form of ideological training. In January 1952, the framework for the new

19 NAH F. 276, u. 53/233. 63. Report about the session of the PC. Budapest, May 25, 1955.
20 NAH F. 276, u. 54/400. 61–62. Report about the session of the Secretariat. Budapest, May 10, 1956.
21 NAH F. 276, u. 54/383. 12., 30–32. Report about the session of the Secretariat. Budapest, October 7, 1955.
22 NAH F. 288, u. 5/11. 90–91. Report about the session of the PC of the MSZMP. December 9, 1956.
23 NAH F. 288, u. 5/97–98. 212. Report about the session of the PC of the MSZMP. Budapest, September 30, 1958.
24 NAH F. 276, u. 54/98. 28–29. Report about the session of the Secretariat. Budapest, April 29, 1950.

system was decided upon: 23,000 people had received Party education in 1951, which was set to be increased to 24,000 by 1952. Only 480 were directed to the Party College, with a larger percentage of students slated for schools lasting only a few weeks or months.[25] In July 1952, considerations were made regarding the use of the methods of the Party College of the CPSU to elevate the training to the level of state colleges, but shortly afterwards it was realised that a rigid adoption of the Muscovite practice was not capable of remedying the existing problems.[26]

Later, an ambition to achieve genuine scientific quality emerged. To this end, departments were bolstered with academics and professors described as 'the most qualified theoretical cadres'.[27] In September 1955, the directorate of the College proposed the establishment of a Scientific Council, following the Soviet example, where theoretical and methodological issues, as well as curricula, training programmes, and departmental reports would be discussed. The goal was for the Council to possess the authority to approve candidates' dissertations[28] and to allow the aspirants[29] to defend their theses within the College.[30] However, the latter item of the proposal was first removed from the Secretariat's agenda[31] (presumably considered as unrealistic) and was missing from their subsequent decision.[32]

The so-called 'Party aspirancy' was introduced, which would (in principle) have provided 'highly qualified' cadres with the necessary preparation for senior positions. Compared to state higher education, the College attempted to support its own aspiring students by offering language training, including the compulsory study of Russian and two optional 'Western languages' (although the latter was eventually abolished[33]), as well as preparation for candidates' dissertations.

---

25 NAH F. 276, 54/178. 21–23. Report about the session of the Secretariat. January 30, 1952.

26 NAH F. 276, u. 53/128. 23. Report about the session of the PC. July 27, 1953.

27 NAH F. 276, u. 54/367. 74. Report about the session of the Secretariat. May 20, 1955.

28 The 'Candidate of Sciences' degree (based on the Soviet model) was established by the Council of Ministers in 1950, transferring the authority to award doctorates from universities to the Hungarian Academy of Sciences. In 1951, the use of former academic titles was abolished and the 'Doctor of Sciences' degree was introduced (Kozári, 2017, pp. 150–151). For further details, see the writings on scientific recruitment in the edited volume by Németh, Garai, and Szabó (2016).

29 'Aspirant' refers to a person who has attended a doctoral training (1950. évi 44. törvényerejű rendelet 2. §).

30 NAH F. 276, u. 54/380. 114–115. Report about the session of the Secretariat. September 27, 1955.

31 NAH F. 276, u. 54/380. 10. Report about the session of the Secretariat. September 30, 1955.

32 NAH F. 276, u. 54/383. 6. Report about the session of the Secretariat. October 17, 1955.

33 NAH F. 276, u. 54/383. 4. Report about the session of the Secretariat. October 17, 1955.

Individual tutoring was provided by Soviet professors working at the College and Hungarian lecturers who held Candidate degrees.[34]

Status and connection to ideological training in higher education

The training at the College emphasised the cultivations of 'communist vigilance' and 'partyist attitudes', mainly through the study of the history of the USSR and Leninist-Stalinist literature. From this perspective, the authorities sought to transform the College into a centre for all Party education: the materials from the lectures given here were to be used at all levels of Party schooling. In addition, the College's departments were also involved in the planning of the organisation and overseeing the ideological education within the Marxism-Leninism departments at universities.[35]

Originally, the College and its graduates lacked a legally formalised status. This issue was raised in 1952, leading to a decision to award students with a 'state diploma' starting from the following academic year[36] (although this was not legitimised by the Ministry of Public Education) in order to emphasise the academic nature of the institute. At the beginning of 1954 the matter was revisited, resulting in a decision for the school to be developed into a 'college of university standard'.[37] However, no decision was made requiring students to take a state examination in Marxism-Leninism and one other optional subject before being awarded a state diploma equivalent to a university degree,[38] a proposal slated for May 1954.[39] It was not until March 1956 that was it decided the institution would be classified as a college instead of a university, but would still be authorised to issue a 'state diploma'.[40] The Council of Ministers later clarified that a diploma

34 NAH F. 276, u. 54/383. 30–32. Report about the session of the Secretariat. October 7, 1955.

35 NAH F. 276, u. 53/37. 4. Report about the session of the PC. Budapest, October 3, 1949.; NAH F. 276, u. 54/286. 28–31. Report about the session of the Secretariat. Budapest, January 19, 1954.

36 NAH F. 276, u. 54/202. 25. Report about the session of the Secretariat. Budapest, July 24, 1952.

37 NAH F. 276, u. 53/162. 35. Report about the session of the PC. Budapest, March 8, 1954.

38 NAH F. 276, u. 53/162. 34. Report about the session of the PC. Budapest, February 19, 1954.

39 NAH F. 276, u. 53/162. 3–4. Report about the session of the PC. Budapest, March 8, 1954.

40 NAH F. 276, u. 53/278. 112. Report about the session of the PC. Budapest, March 28, 1956.; NAH F. 276, u. 53/278. 9. Report about the session of the PC. Budapest, March 29, 1956.

obtained from the College should be considered equivalent to a diploma of the state colleges.[41] (Later, teachers at primary and secondary state schools who had obtained a diploma through a state examination at the College were classified as 'teachers with a college degree'.)[42]

Candidates in the higher Party education

As planned in 1949, the schooling of leading and mid-level cadres was to start in the autumn. The one-year College aimed to prepare heads and deputies of the central departments of Party organisations, the heads of subdivisions, members of the county secretariats, and the leading functionaries of mass organisations and the state apparatus, while the two-year College was tasked with training educational and other propagandist[43] cadres. The objective for all of the senior functionaries was to complete the one-year College (or equivalent extracurricular training) in the next 3 years, and for all middle functionaries to complete three or five months of school (or equivalent extracurricular training) in two years. A total of 3,000 students[44] were to be sent to higher party education, with 300 of them expected to graduate from the Party Colleges over two years.[45]

In 1952, the need for longer-term planning of the party school system reforms became apparent. In the period between 1952 and 1956, around 6,000 independent functionaries and staff from 'certain sections' of the state and mass organisations

41 10/1956. (IV. 24.) M. T. számú rendelet a pártfőiskolai oklevél képesítő jellegéről. The higher education structure of the examined period can be considered transitional in several respects, as it inherited many characteristics from the pre-1945 era. However, it acquired a new character following World War II, especially after 1949. During the period under review, colleges primarily differed from universities on the basis of their shorter training periods and more practical (less theoretical-academic) nature. It should be noted that a clearer delineation of the functions and roles of these types of institutions became clearer after 1961. For a more detailed examination of the transformation of higher education during this period, see Garai (2015, 2016) and Ladányi (2003).

42 A Művelődésügyi Minisztérium 1030/1958. számú bér- és munkaügyi tájékoztatója.

43 Propagandists were responsible for training functionaries working in various fields, including agitators (Huhák, 2016, p. 85).

44 It should be noted, however, that these figures represent a somewhat more realistic picture compared to the numbers communicated in the press in May 1949, which reported 50,000 managerial workers and 40,000 upper cadres to be trained under the first five-year plan (Kovács, 1982).

45 NAH F. 276, u. 53/37. 2. Report about the session of the PC. Budapest, October 6, 1949.

were required to participate in higher party education. Around 500–600 of them had to complete the two-year (and later extended to three-year) Party College.

Due to increasing demand, the admission quota for the College was increased from 150 to 180 by the autumn of 1953. To accommodate those unable to attend the full-time, part-time courses were also offered.[46] By 1954, this number was reduced to 160 and later to 100.[47] The five-year long correspondence course began in 1956, and was viewed as an innovation for being open to applications (advertised in the Party papers). The CL and Party committees nominated approximately 130 candidates, but the call for applications resulted in around 350 replies.[48]

After data collection and the deletion of redundant entries, 785 remained in the personal data table, with their age distribution illustrated in Graph 1. Despite the age restrictions, it can be seen that there was a wide age range among the students attending the Party School. The age group between 26 and 34 was the most represented, making up two-thirds of all the candidates.

Graph 1: The age distribution of applicants (N = 785) to the Party College between 1952 and 1956 (own editing).

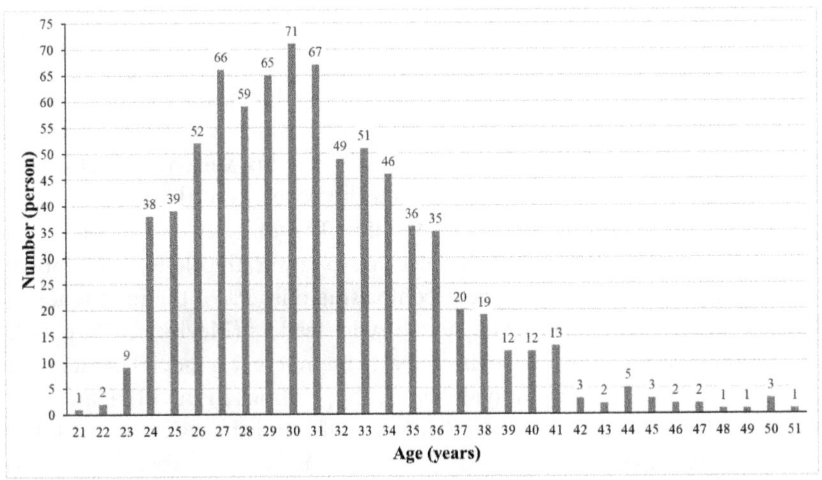

46 NAH F. 276, u. 54/206. 14. Report about the session of the Secretariat. Budapest, August 13, 1952.

47 NAH F. 276, u. 54/302. 69. Report about the session of the Secretariat. Budapest, March 6, 1954.

48 NAH F. 276, u. 54/401. 82. Report about the session of the Secretariat. Budapest, May 30, 1956.

The other segment of the data examined was the year of entry into the MKP or the MDP, with the results shown in Graph 2.

Graph 2: The frequency distribution of candidates (N = 785) to the Party College between 1952 and 1956 (own editing)

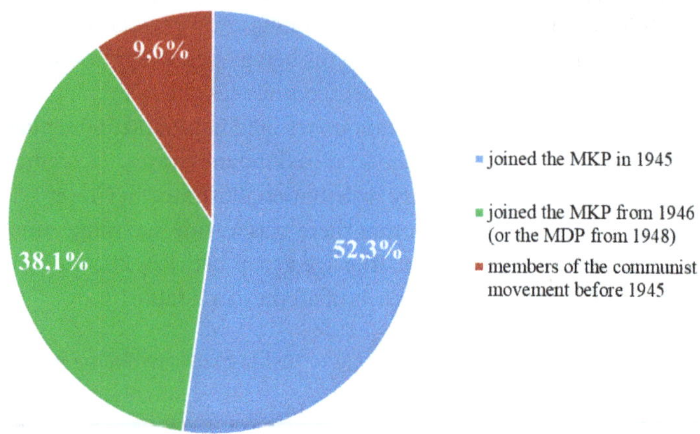

Concerning the pre-1945 party members, it is worth nothing that, in contrast to the Party of Communists in Hungary (KMP), which had enacted the 'red terror' of the Hungarian Soviet Republic in 1919, the 'Muscovites' returning from emigration in the USSR envisioned the progress of the movement in line with Stalin's 'nationalist' pseudo-politics. This difference in vision led to substantial antagonisms until the MDP came to power: the old KMP members were marginalised within the party, comprising only 3% of the functionaries in 1952 and a mere 0.7% of the party district leaders (Mevius, 2005, p. 86). The representation of former coalition party members (e.g., social democrats) was 4.4%. Although many individuals sought positions in the MDP after the merger of the Social Democratic Party (SZDP) and the MKP in 1948, the 'cadre sheets' detailing the candidates' backgrounds had to specifically note former party membership, while the sheets of former SZDP members (along with those who joined after 1945) had to be treated separately. This strict regulation predicted further career paths for some, as a trusted party position could only be obtained with a 'good reputation', despite the fact that 67% of the party consisted of non-Communist sympathisers in 1949 (Gyarmati, 1991; Huszár, 2005).

Selection conditions and recruitment criteria

When the PC organised the College, the target number was increased from 75 to 80. There were 20 missing participants according to the minutes of the meetings, an issue that had to be dealt with based on the criteria discussed during these sessions.[49] These specific aspects, however, are not known due to a lack of available sources.[50]

From the 1950/1951 academic year, an entrance examination was introduced for which those with candidate status were required to take a month's paid leave to prepare. For those from working-class or peasant backgrounds who had not completed four years of secondary school, a two-month summer preparatory course was organised which covered basic skills such as spelling and mathematics, along with the necessary political literature. The completion of this course was deemed sufficient for admission in addition to a 'formal entrance exam' that had to be taken thereafter.[51] According to expectations, mainly 'educated workers' would be sent to the Party College; a selection would be carried out among these students 'with great care' to ensure that 80% of them would be Party functionaries.[52] In this academic year, eight students were removed due to their 'fascist past' among other reasons. Furthermore, 16 second-year students were not recommended to continue to the specialisation course due to their 'incapability for higher-level propaganda work'. Six first-year students were also recalled. Nevertheless, the directorate assessed the selection of the Colleges' students as generally satisfactory and commended the work of the school cadre department established during the year for their investigation of students backgrounds and identification of 'enemy elements'.[53]

In addition to categorising origins, there were also special procedures for indicating party membership. In all cases, it was mandatory to note whether candidates had previously belonged to another party, had joined the communist

49 NAH F. 276, u. 53/37. 2. Report about the session of the PC. Budapest, October 6, 1949.

50 As only draft minutes of meetings were initially written which do not include the text of the debates on the agenda items, it is difficult to reconstruct what the exact agenda of the session was (T. Varga, 2005, p. 7).

51 NAH F. 276, u. 54/98. 29. Report about the session of the Secretariat. Budapest, April 29, 1950.

52 NAH F. 276, u. 54/98. 4. Report about the session of the Secretariat. Budapest, May 3, 1950.

53 NAH F. 276, u. 54/153. 8–10. Report about the session of the Secretariat. Budapest, July 23, 1951.

movement later, or had become a member of the MKP after 1945 (Gyarmati, 1991). Those with Yugoslav origins or family connections, prior membership in the SZDP, or those lacking 'reassuring clarification' of possible 'kulak origin' were categorised as having 'disputed status'.

The decisions made in 1952 were aimed at raising the quality of the students by regulating the admission standards. From the following school year onwards, students lacking primary school qualification were only admitted under exceptional circumstances. Only a 'very small' percentage of individuals from lower middle-class backgrounds were allowed to enrol, and the age range for candidates was narrowed between 22 and 40, although exceptions were allowed (in principle) in well-justified cases.[54] The age limit was soon raised to 24, with the condition that younger candidates could only be sent to the College on the basis of approval.[55] In addition, the CL's proposing departments often made retrospective requests for certain students to be recalled, transferred to another level of party school, or admitted to certain courses (despite the restrictive conditions in effect) in the case of 'good cause'.[56]

The most rigorous admission criteria were implemented for the aspirant training organised in 1955. The DPMO was only permitted to recommend candidates with at least five years of party membership, a university or party college degree (i.e., a degree equivalent to a college diploma in the case of the latter), and leadership experience in a Party, mass organisation, or state function. They were also required to pass entrance examinations in Philosophy and the History of the USSR at a 'university level'.[57]

Workplaces presented challenges both in the selection and distribution of students. On the one hand, some workplaces were reluctant to send staff to training courses; on the other hand, when graduates were distributed, only a few of them were employed by the hosting Party organs, thereby filtering out all but the most talented individuals, as these organs wanted to employ only the 'good cadres'. The Party apparatus wrote to the Secretariat on many occasions, detailing issues with the schooling and distribution system. The most prevalent complaint, whether

54 NAH F. 276, u. 54/199. 4–5. Report about the session of the Secretariat. Budapest, July 25, 1952.

55 NAH F. 276, u. 54/201. 5. Report about the session of the Secretariat. Budapest, July 9, 1952.

56 NAH F. 276, u. 55/214. 7. Report about the session of the PC. Budapest, September 15, 1952.

57 NAH F. 276, u. 54/383. 32. Report about the session of the Secretariat. Budapest, October 7, 1955.

real or perceived, was the reassignment of an exceptional cadre to another organ, while the original body itself faced 'a serious cadre shortage'; there were complaints that an individual had been 'sent to school to strengthen the body', or that a 'replacement was not possible'. Conversely, there were also instances where an organ itself reported that it had prevented senior functionaries from being sent to school due to a perceived lack of 'the necessary political skills'.

Qualifications and critiques of student skills and teaching

In their reports on the academic years, the CL departments did not provide any data illustrating the quality of education (e.g., exam results) apart from subjective observations. These included comments on the inadequacy of students' prior education, political experience, and the poor 'literacy level' of the students, which made it difficult to appoint them in suitable propagandist positions.

After the 1954/1955 school year, there was a noted improvement in the theoretical and political quality of the program, which could be related to the significantly tighter admission requirements. Candidates were now required to pass 'secondary school level' entrance examinations in Hungarian language, Hungarian history, and Geography before being approved by the Secretariat. However, this did not mean that senior functionaries attending the College could effectively manage their duties after graduation. Many were still admitted to the school with only the minimum required four-year secondary school qualification, and a preparatory course remained as an option for those who did not meet this criterion.[58]

The central authorities were dissatisfied with the preparation of teachers, both in terms of their qualifications and their work (although in many cases problems stemmed from organisational deficits and poor decisions). Oftentimes, lecturers were fresh graduates, many of whom had no teaching experience. In some years, a third of the teaching staff were under the age of 25 and possessed less ideological training than what they were tasked to teach, while half of the staff were completing their secondary school correspondence courses in parallel with their work at the College.[59] To address this problem, young teachers hired at the school initially employed as assistants for a year before being allowed to teach independently.[60] Lecturers was occasionally recruited from among young university graduates,

58 NAH F. 276, u. 53/162. 35–36. Report about the session of the PC. Budapest, March 8, 1954.

59 NAH F. 276, u. 53/128. 23. Report about the session of the PC. Budapest, July 27, 1953.

60 NAH F. 276, u. 53/155. 52. Report about the session of the PC. Budapest, January 20, 1954.

but the primary concern with these individuals was often their 'lack of Party experience'.[61]

The College also faced a relatively high turnover rate among lecturers, a common issue in cadre recruitment in general (Ring et al., 2020). Many lecturers were requested by other Party organs to fill various posts even before they had been appointed to the College. In addition, a number of teachers considered unfit were dismissed by the Secretariat each year, despite recurring staff shortages.

From 1954, an increasing number of the College's teachers applied for state (correspondence) post-graduate aspirant courses to achieve a 'higher ideological standard' in their teaching. In order to prepare for the aspirant exam and write their candidate's dissertation, they were provided with independence, and some of them were granted the title by the Hungarian Academy of Sciences.[62] Dissertation themes were submitted by the DPMO and approved by the Secretariat.

To improve quality, only select expert groups were involved, while public higher education and academia were excluded. For example, the strengthening of the Department of the History of the CPSU at the College was envisioned through the recruitment of Soviet professors, graduates of Soviet universities, and aspirants in Marxism-Leninism; heads of CL departments and deputy ministers were also considered for involvement.[63]

Summary

This paper provided insight into the micro-level reality of the operation (or rather 'running') of the Party College of the MDP based on the limited available archival corpus, and in this respect it did not aim for a complete account. It did, however, seek to highlight that the school was the scene for constant experimentation, especially since the teaching of ideology lacked both external and internal points of reference in the party school system for teaching Marxism-Leninism or in the parallel higher education ideology faculties. The problems related to the number and quality of teaching staff further complicated the training. This is likely the main reason why the College never attained the standards of state higher education (at most, it was granted similar rights to award diplomas by law or Party decrees).

61 NAH F. 276, u. 54/251. 21. Report about the session of the Secretariat. Budapest, July 13, 1953.

62 NAH F. 276, u. 54/376. 110. Report about the session of the Secretariat. Budapest, September 5, 1955.

63 NAH F. 276, u. 53/155. 52. Report about the session of the PC. Budapest, January 20, 1954.

The recruitment mechanisms at the College essentially mapped the conceptual framework of the MDP's general approach, with categorisation based on social status, the exclusion of academic performance, and the indexing of life histories. For new cadres, largely composed of young individuals, graduation from party schools presented a key opportunity for career advancement. However, the lack of minimum educational requirements to effectively perform in leadership position and exclusion based on social background severely limited their career development opportunities (Gyarmati, 1991; Ring et al., 2020), increasing the dissatisfaction of the Party leadership. Furthermore, the cadre system, based on planned instructions, struggled to deal with problems arising from personal attachments or unplanned work in lower-level party organisations as well as the destructive attitude towards the possibility of further training that this rigidity implied.

Regarding the selection of students, it can be observed that while the Party leadership established a framework for subordinate departments and the directorate of the College in the compilation of the lists of proposed functionaries, this framework was often overwritten by the leaders themselves. It became apparent that the decision-makers, partly as a result of their own ideological constraints, aimed to form a 'new elite' from social classes ill-suited to this role, either in terms of their background or their attitudes. Ongoing dissatisfaction among the organisations involved in the sending and receiving of cadres and the declarative role of the central bodies in regard to how the capabilities of cadres were viewed revealed a scenario in which few well-qualified individuals were recognised as truly competent. As such, the Party organs showed a willingness to make a serious effort in incorporating these individuals into their own apparatus.

Bibliography

Bara, Zs. (2007). Az „ismeretlen" prozopográfia. *Neveléstörténet*, *4*(1–2), 234–244.

Bourdieu, P. (2005). The Political Field, the Social Science Field, and the Journalistic Field. In R. Benson, & E. Neveu (Eds.), *Bourdieu and the Journalistic Field* (pp. 29–47). Polity Press.

Broady, D. (2002). French prosopography: Definition and suggested readings. *Poetics*, *30*(5–6), 381–385. https://doi.org/10.1016/S0304-422X(02)00031-1

Engel, P. (2006). Prozopográfia. In I. Bertényi (Ed.), *A történelem segédtudományai* (pp. 33–34). Osiris Kiadó.

Garai, I. (2015). Tudománypolitika és felsőoktatás Magyarországon, 1948–1951. In A. Németh, Zs. H. Biró, & I. Garai (Eds.), *Neveléstudomány és tudományos elit a 20. század második felében* (pp. 165–176). Gondolat Kiadó. https://real.mtak.hu/35462/1/Nevelestudomany_törd_1.pdf

Garai, I. (2016). A magyar felsőoktatás strukturális átalakítási és államosítási kísérletei az 1949–1953 közötti időszakban. In A. Németh, I. Garai, & Z. A. Szabó (Eds.), *Neveléstudomány és pedagógiai kommunikáció a szocializmus időszakában* (pp. 119–160). Gondolat Kiadó. https://real.mtak.hu/39151/1/PTE_Nemeth_javitott.pdf

Golnhofer, E. (2004). *Hazai pedagógiai nézetek 1945–1949*. Iskolakultúra. https://mek.oszk.hu/02400/02445/02445.pdf

Gyarmati, Gy. (1991). A káderrendszer és a rendszer kádere az ötvenes években. *Valóság*, *34*(2), 51–63.

Huhák, H. (2016). Kicsapás a Pártiskoláról: Két fegyelmi ügy a propaganda mikrovilágából. *Kommentár*, *11*(5), 84–99. http://kommentar.info.hu/uploads/2016/5/1582812138.pdf

Huszár, T. (2005). Az elittől a nómenklatúráig: Az intézményesített káderpolitika kialakulása és néhány jellemzője Magyarországon (1945–1989). *Szociológiai Szemle*, *15*(3), 8–69. https://szociologia.hu/dynamic/0503huszar.pdf

Ispán, Á. L. (2021). Parasztkáderek az iskolapadban. *ÚJKOR.HU*. https://ujkor.hu/content/parasztkaderek-az-iskolapadban

Kéri, K. (2001). *Bevezetés a neveléstörténeti kutatások módszertanába*. Műszaki Könyvkiadó.

Kontra, J. (2011). *A pedagógiai kutatások módszertana*. Kaposvári Egyetem. https://mek.oszk.hu/12600/12648/12648.pdf

Kovács M., M. (1982). Közalkalmazottak, 1938–1949. *Valóság*, *25*(9), 41–53.

Kozári, M. (2017). A tudományos minősítés rendszere Magyarországon az 1940-es évek végétől 1960-ig, az új minősítési rendszer stabilizálódásáig. *Múltunk – Politikatörténeti Folyóirat*, *60*(2), 148–198. https://real.mtak.hu/139880/1/kozarim_15_2.pdf

Körösényi, A. (1998). *A magyar politikai rendszer*. Osiris Kiadó.

Ladányi, A. (1995). A felsőoktatási felvételi rendszer történeti alakulása. *Educatio*, *4*(3), 485–500. http://epa.oszk.hu/01500/01551/00074/pdf/EPA01551_education_1995_3_485-500.pdf

Ladányi, A. (2003). A magyar felsőoktatás intézményrendszerének változásai a 20. században. In L. Szögi, & L. Rutkai (Eds.), *Az Egyetemi Könyvtár évkönyvei* (Vol. 11, pp. 177–205). Eötvös Loránd Tudományegyetem Egyetemi Könyvtár. https://library.hungaricana.hu/hu/view/EgyetemiKonyvtarEvkonyvei_11

Matthews, M. (2012). *Education in the Soviet Union: Policies and Institutions since Stalin* (Vol. 9). Routledge.

Mawdsley, E., & Munck, T. (1996). *Számítógép a történettudományban*. Osiris Kiadó.

MDP KV Oktatási Osztály (1948). *A következő láncszem: Elméleti feladataink és a pártoktatás*. N. P.

Mevius, M. (2005). *Agents of Moscow: The Hungarian Communist Party and the Origins of Socialist Patriotism*. Oxford University Press.

Németh, A., & Biró, Zs. H. (2016). A magyar neveléstudomány diszciplína jellemzőinek és kognitív tartalmainak változásai a 20. század második felében. In A. Németh, I. Garai, & Z. A. Szabó (Eds.), *Neveléstudomány és pedagógiai kommunikáció a szocializmus időszakában* (pp. 53–56). Gondolat Kiadó. http://real.mtak.hu/39151/1/PTE_Nemeth_javitott.pdf

Németh, A., Garai, I., & Szabó, Z. A. (Eds.). (2016). *Neveléstudomány és pedagógiai kommunikáció a szocializmus időszakában*. Gondolat Kiadó. https://real.mtak.hu/39151/1/PTE_Nemeth_javitott.pdf

Németh, A., & Szabolcs, É. (2002). A neveléstörténeti kutatások főbb nemzetközi tendenciái, új kutatási módszerei és eredményei. In Z. Báthory, & I. Falus (Eds.), *Tanulmányok a neveléstudomány köréből 2001* (pp. 46–76). Osiris Kiadó. https://real-j.mtak.hu/21514/1/956_940.pdf

Paksa, R. (2013). Prozopográfia vagyis „kollektív biográfiai elemzés". In D. Ballabás (Ed.), *Módszertani tanulmányok* (pp. 7–19). EKF Líceum Kiadó. http://publikacio.uni-eszterhazy.hu/5769/1/7_19_Paksa.pdf

Pukánszky, B., & Németh, A. (1995). *Neveléstörténet*. Nemzeti Tankönyvkiadó.

Ring, O., Kiss, L., & Turnai, A. (2020). Női káderek a Rákosi-korszakban. *Századok*, *154*(1), 107–134. https://epa.oszk.hu/03300/03328/00037/pdf/EPA03328_szazadok_2020_01_107-134.pdf

Roucek, J. S. (1958). Party Control and Education of Party Members in the U.S.S.R. *Slavic and East-European Studies*, *3*(2), 91–103.

Rutland, P. (1993). *The politics of economic stagnation in the Soviet Union: The role of local party organs in economic management*. Cambridge University Press.

Ruzsa, B., Lukovszki, E., Vincze, B., & Garai, I. (2024). Transformation of the scientific institutional settings of education sciences in the decades after the consolidation of the Kádár-regime. In Z. A. Szabó, L. Somogyvári, I. Garai, & A. Németh (Eds.), *Evolving perspectives: The development of Hungarian educational science after 1945* (pp. 27–52). Peter Lang.

Sáska, G. (2021). Az egyenlőség és az elkülönülés oktatáspolitikájának két korszaka Magyarországon. *Educatio*, *30*(3), 479–495. https://doi.org/10.1556/2063.30.2021.3.8

Simon, R. (2000). *Goldziher Ignác: Vázlatok az emberről és a tudósról*. Osiris Kiadó.

Somogyvári, L. (2015). Származási kategóriák és lemorzsolódás a középiskolában (1953–1962). *Neveléstudomány | Oktatás – Kutatás – Innováció*, *3*(3), 56–68. https://ojs.elte.hu/nevelestudomany/article/view/6543/4983

Somogyvári, L., Polyák, Zs., & Németh, A. (2021). Új elméleti keretek a szocialista neveléstudomány vizsgálatára: A politikai vallás. *Magyar Pedagógia*, *121*(1), 85–97. https://doi.org/10.17670/MPed.2021.1.85

Stones, L. (1971). Prosopography. *Daedalus*, *100*(1), 46–79. http://www.jstor.org/stable/20023990

Szabó, Z. A., Garai, I., & Németh, A. (2022). The history of education in Hungary from the mid-19th century to present day. *Paedagogica Historica*, *58*(6), 901–919. https://doi.org/10.1080/00309230.2022.2090849

Szakolczai, A. (2014). *A Tóth Ilona és társai per komplex vizsgálata*. Doktori disszertáció. Pécsi Tudományegyetem Interdiszciplináris Doktori Iskola. https://pea.lib.pte.hu/bitstream/handle/pea/14974/szakolczai-attila-phd-2015.pdf

T. Varga, Gy. (1998). Adalékok és szempontok a Magyar Dolgozók Pártja hatalmi helyzetéhez. *Múltunk – Politikatörténeti Folyóirat*, *43*(2), 175–182.

T. Varga, Gy. (2005). *Az MDP központi vezetősége, politikai bizottsága és titkársága üléseinek napirendi jegyzékei 1948–1953* (Vol. 1). Magyar Országos Levéltár. https://library.hungaricana.hu/hu/view/MolDigiLib_MOLsegedl_18_1

Verboven, K., Carlier, M., & Dumolyn, J. (2007). A Short Manual to the Art of Prosopography. In K. S. B. Keats-Rohan (Ed.), *Prosopography Approaches and Applications: A Handbook* (pp. 35–69). Linacre College. https://prosopography.history.ox.ac.uk/images/01%20Verboven%20pdf.pdf

Lajos Somogyvári,[1] Zsuzsanna Polyák[2]

Towards a new interpretation framework: Political religion and socialist pedagogy in Hungary

Abstract: In our paper, the concept of political religion serves as a theoretical background, enabling new insights into the development of education sciences in the socialist era, from the late 1960s until the regime change in 1989. Our interpretation is rooted in the analysis of authoritarian and totalitarian political systems, such as Fascism, Nazism, and Communism. We focus on the quasi-religious, ritual elements of socialist pedagogy, presenting how official ideology was transformed through symbols, language, and discursive forms into knowledge-producing and scientific processes. *Magyar Pedagógia* [Hungarian Pedagogy], as a flagship journal and an exemplary forum in the Hungarian scientific space, provided the corpus for analysing this complex phenomenon. The first step in our research design was building a vocabulary to create various categories of political religion. The characteristics of religion and ideology are comparable in several respects: they share similar goals, involve community activities, include ceremonial elements and liturgies, and hold temporal views which establish their universal and specific natures. The journal was analysed using semi-automatic coding with data analysis software that facilitated both quantitative and qualitative examination of extensive bodies of text. The results of the quantitative analysis, including the frequencies and co-occurrences of ideologically charged terminology, revealed the timeline and extent of the ideology's dissemination in professional discourse. By examining this content, the research aims to provide valuable insights into how authoritarian and totalitarian regimes can exert influence over professional discourses and the legacy of such influence in the post-socialist context.

Keywords: political religion, socialist pedagogy, ideology, text mining

1 University of Pannonia, Institute of Education Sciences, Veszprém, Hungary, somogyvari.lajos@htk.uni-pannon.hu

2 Liszt Ferenc Academy of Music, Budapest, Hungary

Introduction

Political religion (PR), as a research tool, allows us to investigate the totalitarian regimes of the 20th century from a unique perspective. This study builds on our previous explorations of the topic. We aimed to apply this key notion to Hungarian education sciences after 1945 (Somogyvári et al., 2021) and to reveal its significance in the new musical culture (Polyák et al., 2021). Furthermore, we sought to establish connections with the Scientific-Technological Revolution (Somogyvári & Polyák, 2022, 2023). The scientifically rooted Marxist-Leninist ideology promoted a deterministic image of the future, mixing seemingly clear principles with a utopian (albeit vague) vision of existing socialism and its ultimate form, ideal communism. Through this logic, politics became sacralised in a secular world (Payne, 2005, p. 172). Different accents and focal points emerged in the evolution of such discourses, including the creation and selection of politically required prefigurations for the socialist present and a desirable future. We begin by sketching the theoretical outline of this approach in the form of a brief research history.

Political religion as an umbrella term is used in various contexts: these include uncovering the historical foundation of US Constitutional Law through a psychoanalytic lens (Richards, 2023), exploring Hungarian patriotism (Nyirkos, 2023), feminist theory (Cheruvallil-Contractor, 2023), or reconciling modern political interventions with moral codes and religious traditions (Gabriel, 2023). These selected examples showcase the adaptability of the concept, highlighting the necessity for a clear definition and limitations in its application. Political religion has a long history, originating in the thoughts of Tocqueville and Burke, who characterised republicanism as a form of sacral nationalism, linking it to the French Revolution (Bourke, 2020). In the turbulent 1930s, a new kind of anthropological revolution emerged, with totalitarian movements (i.e., Fascism, Nazism, and Communism) advocating for a transformation of mankind through the creation of the New Man. It is thus no wonder that the modern form of political religion was developed in 1938 by the German-American philosopher Eric Voegelin (referenced in a selected volume of his works: Voegelin, 2000), who contextualised totalitarianism within the process of secularization. Hans Maier later built on Voegelin's work, initially linking the three political orders to a quasi-religious dimension, where social cohesion is maintained by ideologies of race (blood) and class instead of the Christian tradition. The following year, in 1939, Raymond Aron expanded this description from a liberal viewpoint, incorporating omnipotent ideologies and 'absolute values' (Maier, 2007, p. 10).

The combination of strong ideology and values, coupled with a religious-like fervour in new totalitarian politics and mass mobilization, formed the basis of this concept.

The two decades following the collapse of the bipolar world (the 1990s and 2000s) proved to be a fruitful period for the theory. Emilio Gentile, an Italian history professor, developed the most influential framework of political religion, applying it specifically to Fascism. In his work, he defined the sacralisation of politics based on four different aspects:

1. Ideology reigns supreme, dominated by the 'secular collective entity' (in this case, the Party, which ideally represents the will of the ruling class, i.e., the proletariat).
2. Consequently, individuals are required to subordinate themselves to the moral monopoly of this entity.
3. The system adopts 'a mission of benefit to all humanity,' offering a utopian vision of the past, present, and future.
4. Lastly, the political sphere establishes a liturgical calendar and a 'sacred history' replete with 'symbolic representations' (Gentile, 2006, pp. 138–139).

In our analysis, we aim to uncover the pervasive influence of ideology on scientific discourses, highlighting the aforementioned aspects. Socialist pedagogy can also be viewed through this lens as a type of 'secular collective entity', a blend of imaginations, scientific facts, and legendary figures inseparably intertwined. This synthesis created a unique pedagogical history that incorporated various educational principles that aligned with a collective moral consciousness, standing in contrast with capitalist bourgeois pedagogy.

Gentile emphasised that while political religion can be associated with totalitarian states, civil religion also exists in pluralistic democratic societies, such as the US. However, scholarly attention has predominantly focused on the former, though there has been a noticeable shift in recent years. This trend is reflected in edited volumes such as *Totalitarianism and Political Religions* by Hans Maier (Maier, 2004, 2007; Maier & Schäfer, 2007), as well as the journal *Totalitarian Movements and Political Religions*, launched in 2000 (later renamed *Politics, Religion, and Ideology* in 2011), which exclusively examined non-liberal ideologies (Barry, 2015, p. 627). In this series, political religion is closely associated with the concept of totalitarianism. Hannah Arendt first used the word totalitarianism to describe new forms of government in Nazism and Stalinism (1951). Later, Carl Friedrich and Zbigniew Brzezinski applied totalitarianism (1956) to the same group (Fascist Italy, Nazi Germany, and the Communist Soviet Union); this was similar to Voegelin's earlier application of political religion, albeit in the context of the Cold War era. Terror is an inherent element of these concepts, whereas political religion emphasizes the appealing aspects of these political systems – this distinction may be the primary difference between the two concepts (Polyák et al., 2021, p. 231).

In our study we will adopt Gentile's definition of political religion, while also considering its limitations and critiques. One fundamental criticism targets its generalised view: ideas regarding existing socialism and future communism vary significantly across geographic regions (e.g., the Eastern and Western hemispheres) and are conceptually distinct, as other so-called totalitarian states have developed within unique socio-historical contexts. The pedagogical discourses analysed here will primarily focus on the normative, optimistic portrayals of socialist education from a Hungarian perspective, during a specific period characterised by fluctuating ideological intensity and shifting significance. Consequently, this investigation is intentionally narrow, employing a rigorous methodology to ensure the reliability of the results.

Research questions

Communism, socialism, and Marxism-Leninism carry vastly different meanings and connotations in the Western and Eastern hemispheres. It is deeply paradoxical that "state-driven socialism" in the East attempted to portray a utopian vision (Morgan, 2005, p. 393) even as the existing system and its social imaginaries were always in conflict. Conversely, in Western countries, Marxism-Leninism may still be viewed as a theory of hope and revolutionary justice. These differing perspectives fundamentally shape the understanding of these ideologies. Therefore, it is important to emphasize that our study focuses on the form of socialism that existed in Hungary from the late 1960s until the regime change, including its transformation and eventual dismantling during the 1990s and 2000s.

Our central question is the following: How did the official (e.g., communist Marxist or socialist, depending on the context) ideology appear in educational scientific discourses throughout this period? We will examine these representations from the perspective of political religion theory, focusing on four main features that address these queries:

1. What genres were most influenced by ideological content?
2. Who are the authors of these highly ideologised texts? What are their professional backgrounds?

3. What topics are covered in these highly ideologised texts?
4. How can we characterize the discursive context of the aspects of political religion that are most prominent in the highly ideologised texts?

Methods and sample

The sample for this study included all articles that were published between 1968–2018 in the leading Hungarian academic journal of education science, *Magyar Pedagógia* [Hungarian Pedagogy], regardless of genre (n=2018). A flagship journal such as this one often serves a political function by legitimising and naming research topics and directions, highlighting social issues, and suggesting possible solutions (Iso-Ahola, 2009). In other words, such a platform influences and shapes public discourse as well as the profession itself. In a one-party system, this role is typically much more pronounced than in democratic countries.

The data collection concluded in 2018, but the corpus primarily consists of articles from the 1970s and, to a lesser extent, the 1980s, due to our selection criteria and theoretical framework.

We employed an explanatory sequential mixed methods design (Creswell, 2014), starting with a quantitative, text-mining phase, followed by a qualitative analysis of the outliers identified in the first phase, and incorporating a contextual analysis to understand the institutional and professional backgrounds of the authors who produced the highly ideologized texts (Ignatow & Mihalcea, 2018; Landwehr, 2008).

For the text mining phase, we developed a dictionary based on the theoretical categories of political religion and the outcomes of our earlier pilot studies (Polyák, Somogyvári & Németh, 2021; Polyák, Szabó & Németh, 2021; Somogyvári et al., 2021; Somogyvári & Polyák, 2023). We organised these categories into three main groups: agencies, socio-political imaginaries, and knowledge fields. Each of these groups can be linked to symbolic universes, the highest level of legitimation, which give order to everyday meanings and institutions in a figurative way (Berger & Luckmann, 1966, p. 113), including actors, images, and content. These categories are not only theoretical abstractions, but constitute totalities in that period, representing the super-reality (or transcendency) of the ideology (see Table 1 for the categories).

Table 1: Categories of the analysis (own editing)

Main categories	Categories	Some sub-categories within
Agencies	Party [Communist/ Socialist]	Hungarian Socialist Workers' Party, Hungarian Communist Party, party decree, agitation, propaganda, membership, pedagogues as members, school reform, social and cultural progression, etc.
	Working class	proletariat, the rule of the working class, production, the dictatorship of the proletariat, fight, fighter, conscious, etc.
	Soviet Union	bolshevik, Red Army, example, brother, brotherhood, leader, developed, Central Committee, Communist Party of the Soviet Union, vanguard, etc.
	Other socialist countries	Czechoslovakia, GDR, Poland, Romania, China, Cuba, Angola, Yugoslavia, etc.
	Other non-socialist countries	USA, West Germany, France, UK, Spain, Italy, Vatican, etc.
	Soviet professional	Makarenko, Krupskaya, Pavlov, Lunacharski, Skatkin, Shapovalenko, Medinski, Kairov, Jesipov, Zankov, etc.
	Hungarian professional	László Nagy, Oszkár Fáber, György Lukács, Ferenc Földes, Samu Czabán, László Kardos, etc.
	Other professional	Comenius, Pestalozzi, Rousseau, Gramsci, Shaw, Brecht, Adorno, Marcuse, Sartre, Rudi Dutschke, Henri Wallon, Paul Langevin, Piaget, etc.
	Children	pioneers, youth movement, Communist Youth League, learning youth, working youth, community, celebration, brigades, young workers, student council, etc.

Main categories	Categories	Some sub-categories within
Socio-political imaginaries	Future orientation	peace, peaceful coexistence, progression, democracy, new society, struggle, modern education, heaven, liberation, etc.
	Enemies	Fascism, Hitler, imperialism, capitalism, irredentism, reactionist, bourgeoise, West, clericalism, Horthy, conservativism, religion, landowners, etc.
	Sins	oppression, individualism, cosmopolitism, Herbartian, pessimistic, revisionist, decadent, anti-democratic, consumption, Western influences, personal cult, etc.
	Virtues	moral, work, optimism, socialist patriotism, well-rounded men, harmonious individual, ideal, communist men, future men, consciousness, progressive thinking, etc.
	"Prophets"	Marx, Engels, Lenin, sacral texts
Knowledge fields	Celebrations	rituals, the Hungarian Soviet Republic, the Great October Socialist Revolution, 1917, May 1, April 4, Liberation Day, November 7, pioneers' inauguration, rally, parade, Lenin corner, March 15, 1945, the birth of Lenin, people's democracy, etc.
	Socialist pedagogy	reducing curricula, polytechnic education, working education, modern pedagogy, modern culture, communist education, overall development, political education, overload, Marxist-Leninist pedagogy, socialist consciousness, etc.
	Science and technology	progressions, space age, competition, scientifically established principles, world order, airplanes, spaceships, rockets, chemistry, factories, optimism, surpass, etc.
	Community/ communitarianism	nationalisation, collective, community, movement, masses, cooperatives, egalitarianism, public opinion, development, collective behaviour, etc.
	Internationalism	brotherhood, Camp, colonialism, liberation, Third World, postcolonial countries, imperialism, imperialist countries, solidarity, union, festival, new democracies, etc.
	Ideology	dialectic, liberation, revolution, communism, Leninism, materialism, class struggle, progression, morals, propaganda, objective principles, cultural revolution, worldview, politics, etc.

We used MAXQDA software for the analysis, ranking the papers in the sample based on the prevalence of ideological content, which was determined by the average relative frequencies of expressions in our dictionary. This enabled us to identify highly ideologised papers. In the qualitative phase, we examined prominent discourses in the selected papers and researched the professional backgrounds of the authors to provide a broader contextual understanding.

"Ideological" genres

Table 2 shows the average relative frequency of political religion terminology across genres and the categories with the highest values. The high ranking of the 'Readers' comments', 'Anniversary', and 'Obituary' sections' on the list is attributable to their short length and repeated use of such terminology, which resulted in a higher average relative frequency value. Journal reviewers primarily selected pedagogical periodicals from socialist countries (e.g., Soviet Union, Czechoslovakia, the GDR, or Poland) or interpreted Western journals from a Marxist-Leninist perspective, highlighting the shortcomings of capitalist education systems. Conversely, scientific papers, which ranked 11th, reached their peak in 1970, coinciding with the 100th anniversary of the birth of Lenin. This suggests that professional discourses may be more independent of ideological influence compared to genres related to memory/commemoration and personal opinion. These latter genres are mostly communicative performances with conventional settings and norms (Bathia, 1993) – their value is represented by the author's position and potential connections to the community.

Table 2: Frequency of political religion in different genres (own editing)

Genre	Average relative frequency of political religion	Categories with the highest values
Readers' comments	0,0818	ideology
Anniversary	0,0575	ideology, future orientation
Obituary	0,0473	ideology, Soviet Union
Journal Review	0,0405	ideology
Panorama	0,0384	children, ideology
News	0,0383	children, ideology
Book review	0,0350	children, ideology
Review [other]	0,0338	children
Document	0,0310	ideology

Genre	Average relative frequency of political religion	Categories with the highest values
Editorial	0,0309	ideology
Scientific paper	0,0304	children
Diary	0,0261	children, ideology
Interview	0,0078	Soviet professional
Bibliography	0,0018	"Prophets"

Authors and backgrounds

We initially selected the 20 papers with the highest average relative frequencies of PR content for a qualitative discourse analysis. However, since the term "community" was coded both for under the category of Children ("communities of children") and the general category of Community, this led to the overrepresentation of "community" as a topic. To address this, we excluded these categories and selected a new set of the 20 highest-ranking papers for review.

Graph 1: Articles and the average political religion content.

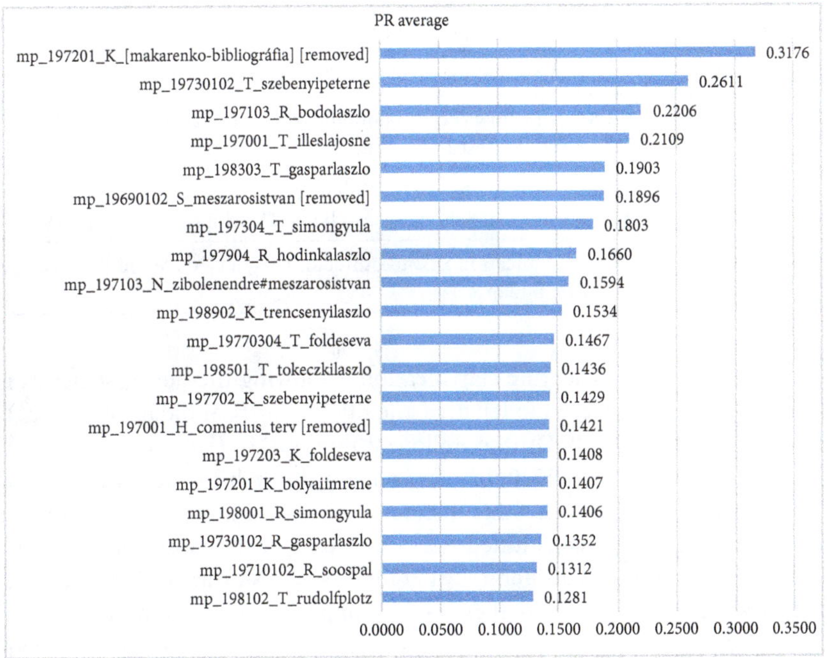

Table 3: Authors and affiliations (own editing)

Author	Workplace/affiliation at the time of publishing
Bodó, László	Deputy director (National Pedagogical Institute, Budapest)
Bólyai, Imréné	Retired associate professor (Budapest)
Földes, Éva	Doctor of education science, college professor; later: senior research fellow
Gáspár, László	DSc of education science, director (Szentlőrinc)
Hodinka, László	Senior research fellow (National Pedagogical Library and Museum, Budapest)
Illés, Lajosné	Deputy department director (National Pedagogical Library and Museum)
Mészáros, István	Assistant professor (Eötvös Loránd University, Budapest)
Plötz, Rudolf	DSc of education science; senior research fellow (GDR Academy of Pedagogy, Berlin)
Simon, Gyula	College professor, executive secretary of the Hungarian Pedagogical Association
Soós, Pál	Assistant professor (Debrecen)
Szebenyi, Péterné	Assistant professor (College of Physical Education, Budapest)
Tőkéczki, László	Research fellow (Eötvös Loránd University, Faculty of Humanities, Research Group on Education History, Budapest)
Trencsényi, László	Senior research fellow (National Pedagogical Institute, Department of School Research and Development, Budapest)
Zibolen, Endre	DSc of Education Science, director (Higher Education Research Centre, Budapest)

In the Eastern Bloc, scientific classification (following the Soviet structure) differed from the Western model: here, the title of CSc (Candidate of Science) was equivalent to the PhD level, followed by the DSc (Doctor of Science) (Kestere & Stonkuviene, 2020, p. 77). Looking through the list of names in Table 3, we can distinguish three distinct professional groups. Historians of education and culture constituted the largest part, with five scholars associated with this field (László Bodó, Éva Földes, István Mészáros, Gyula Simon, and László Tőkéczki). Despite their varying impacts and positions, the size of this group suggests significant implications. In this sense, ideology remained in the past, and was transmitted as a cultural heritage into the 1970s and 1980s, necessitating its reinvention and revitalisation. The second fraction includes scholars who were interested in the youth movement and community education, such as Péterné Szebenyi, László Gáspár, or László Trencsényi. Each of these individuals pursued this topic for different reasons: Gáspár and Trencsényi were involved in experimental and new directions; Péterné Szebenyi approached the field from a moral perspective. Finally, librarians are included, representing authors who played an important role in scientific communication and knowledge dissemination, including Lajosné Illés and László Hodinka.

Topics and discursive contexts

The genre distribution of the selected papers included seven scientific papers, five panoramas, six book reviews, one review and one piece of news. Out of these 20 papers, three were deemed unsuitable for qualitative review (specifically, one bibliography and two short news pieces, marked as [removed] on Graph 1) and were thus excluded from the sample for the thematic analysis phase. Of the remaining papers, six were theoretical, one was theoretical with a summary of empirical research, eight were historical, and two were conference reviews (i.e., summaries of historical and theoretical papers). The historical papers were dedicated to prominent communists such as Lenin and Paul Langevin, examining the history of education through the lens of Marx's theory of historical materialism. The theoretical writings discussed tasks and challenges in education relevant to socialist patriotism and proletarian internationalism, moral education, the development of a well-rounded personality, class struggle, and comparisons of the educational policies and curricula of Western and Socialist countries. The book reviews featured monographs from three Hungarian authors, two books from Mario Alighiero Manacorda, an Italian Marxist, and one by Georges Snyders, a French Marxist.

Empirical research studies are notably absent from the list, which spannned from 1968 to 1989. This absence was particularly evident for those papers not focusing on ideologically relevant topics, where empirical research papers generally exhibited low PR values (albeit not zero). This suggests that the general policy of "de-ideologization" during the Kádár era (1956–1989), which affected everyday life, also influenced scientific discussions as well. The tacit acceptance of the Marxist-Leninist framework as the only scientifically valid approach (cf. "naturalisation of the discourse"; Landwehr, 2008) made it unnecessary to explicitly affirm allegiance to the ideology.

Among the remaining 17 papers, we identified four dominant themes:

1. Reinterpretation attempts of Marxism-Leninism to suit contemporary challenges
2. Moral education
3. Anti-church and anti-capitalism sentiments directed at Western countries
4. Criticism of Western Marxism

Reinterpretation attempts of Marxism-Leninism

The "correct" reinterpretation attempts of Marxism-Leninism became a pressing issue in an era when the shortcomings of existing regimes became more and more evident from the late 1970s. This is apparent in the rapid change in tone observed in the scholarly discourse:

- 1970: "The Soviet Union is now entering a new period in its history, the transition from socialism to communism"[3] (Illés, 1970, p. 26)
- 1977: "far from being communism, but for the time being only in a society striving towards advanced socialism" (Illés, 1977, p. 356)
- 1983: "the socialist society in the different countries of communism is at 'raw' or 'political' stage; the 'positive' stage, which is the free and unconstrained law of the development of each individual, is not within the reach of the generations living today" (Gáspár, 1983, p. 225)

However, rather than representing a departure from ideology, these shifts merely frame the desired historical outcome into a more distant future and examine present results in relation to that vision: "*the guiding criterion for scientific evaluation of existing socialism is whether or not it is objectively a step towards communism. The 'basic norm' of socialist social construction is rapprochement with communism*" (Gáspár, 1983, p. 224). Thus, all actions and outcomes are to be evaluated based on their contribution to the overarching Communist mission.

Criticism in the discourse is typically aimed at the practical application of ideas rather than at the ideological foundations of the regime. Attempts at reinterpretation are strongly connected to the "prophets" of the ideology: Marx and his most worthy successor, Lenin ("*Lenin was the most erudite, the firmest and consistent Marxist, the greatest exponent of Marx's teachings*"; Illés, 1970, p. 26). The authors also emphasised the importance of reading the original Marxist-Leninist literature to understand their enduring messages in a manner that contributed to myth-building.

3 Translations from the Hungarian were done by the authors.

Most papers are more subtle in glorifying the prophets of Marxism-Leninism, portraying them as bearers of ultimate truth who offer a *total worldview,* as well as *moral and practical guidance* to their followers. This illustrates the regimes' efforts to preserve the ideological totalitarianism on which the very existence of the regime depended. Even in times of increasingly obvious crisis, it remained necessary to refer back to fundamental ideas, which provide the "correct" path to solutions.

Moral education and the "new man"

Morality is defined as *"secular, but not simply based on general human principles, but on the principles of Marxism"* (Szebenyi, 1973, p. 144) and is a core question for the totalitarian worldview, which can only function if all under its rule believe in and work towards it. Illés (1970) reinforces this point using Lenin's writings, arguing that *"the moral regeneration of a society [...] starts from the concrete tasks of building a communist society"* (pp. 31–32). Thus, morality is defined as anything that contributes to the Communist mission.

Most of the papers in the sample discuss the historical development of communist moral education, portraying the current state as superior to both historical precedents in socialist countries and contemporary capitalist ones. However, less is mentioned regarding the components of communist education. One notable aspect is the integration of *socialist patriotism* with *proletarian internationalism,* highlighted in the review of the Proceedings of the III International Symposium on the Teaching of History (Bodó, 1971).

Indirect moral guidelines *"for all workers of science, for all advocates of progress"* (Földes, 1973, p. 359) can be found in papers commemorating the 100th birth anniversaries of Nadezhda Krupskaya (1969), Vladimir Lenin (1870), French scientist Paul Langevin (1872), as well as through criticisms of alternative approaches.

Krupskaya is depicted as a devoted advocate for socialist humanism, with a strong ideological-political commitment to the socialist social system, viewed as the historically most favourable environment for human fulfilment (Mészáros, 1969). The selected sample includes reports on two memorial conferences (one in Hungary in 1969 and one in the Soviet Union in 1989) on Krupskaya (Mészáros, 1969; Trencsényi, 1989). It is noteworthy that even the 1989 report – despite its ironical tone – describes Krupskaya as *"a thinker informed by rigorous methodology and European education"* (Trencsényi, 1989, p. 191) while dismissing the "historical icon and example" narrative that was prevalent in 1969 Hungary and was still prominent among school teachers in the Soviet Union in 1989.

We also learn that physicist Paul Langevin's scientific journey led him to embrace communism, despite little being written on his scientific research itself. The text predominantly highlights that his dedication to communism through his work and personal tribulations are what he is to be remembered for. A number of quotes describing Langevin are provided: he was *"an ardent democrat in politics and a progressive thinker in science"*, and *"consistently fought for human rights, against all oppression and injustice"*, *"advocated for a peaceful future for humanity"* and *"enthusiastically welcomed the Russian Revolution of 1905"*; *"from the very beginning, he was an opponent of idealist scientists, physicists and philosophers"*, and *"stressed that communists have the highest moral values and that he embraced their ideals"* (Földes, 1972).

Meanwhile, Lenin is depicted as a figure who *"is more alive than those alive today"* (Illés, 1970, p. 26) and *"affirmed that Marxism was the only correct revolutionary theory"*. Furthermore, he *"fought for the objective economic and social and, at the same time, intellectual and moral foundations of the new man"*. The communist *"new man unites within himself the great cultural energies"* and is a well-rounded person with a sentiment of social solidarity as well as emotional and moral culture.

The concept of a *well-rounded personality* also comes up in the context of moral and polytechnic education. It is claimed that *"people who know how to do everything"* (Illés, 1977, p. 355) could overcome the labour division that Communists regard as the "original sin" and aim to eradicate. By 1977, it had become apparent that this goal could not be achieved in the foreseeable future; nonetheless, educators were still advised to seek out the best methods to strive toward this ideal.

Moral education in Western countries, namely England and West Germany, is criticised for transmitting the *"idealistic, irrational moral value system of religious faith"* (Szebenyi, 1973, p. 272) by *"deducing from Christian ethics the general and natural rules of human coexistence and the humanism-based theory of love"* (p. 276). By anchoring morality in religious beliefs, Western schools do not *"educate for humane sobriety, as those involved believe, but rather for subordination to a dogma of faith, which develops voluntarist, stubbornly intrusive traits"* (Plötz, 1981, p. 172). In these papers, questions of morality and ethics are inherently linked to anti-church and anti-capitalist sentiments.

Anti-church and anti-capitalism sentiments directed at Western countries

Among the traditional enemies of Marxism-Leninism (i.e., the imperialists, capitalists, bourgeoisie, and the church), the "church" is mentioned most frequently in the sample, almost twice as often as "capitalists". The separation of the Church from schooling and the nationalisation of schools are recurrent issues in historical overviews (Simon, 1973, Szebenyi, 1973; Tőkéczki, 1985) and were included in the critiques of capitalist contexts as discussed above.

The historical papers mainly serve to legitimise the current socialist regime's strictly state-run educational system by depicting church-run schools as obsolete and feudalistic. They often highlight the poor infrastructure of these schools (e.g. the lack of heating and textbooks – which was hardly unusual or unique to church-run schools during and after WW2) and frame the nationalisation of schools as the final step in an inevitable historical process.

Plötz (1985) employs rather antagonistic rhetoric in his comparison of curricula between West and East Germany, reflecting deep ideological tensions. He suggests that his opponents criticise the socialist education system for issues that are, in fact, present in their own practices. Specifically, Plötz argues that East German schools empower workers through scientific and technical progress under socialist conditions, while *"the bourgeois ideologues of the FRG* [Federal Republic of Germany] *are at pains to prove that the educational ideal of socialist society is illusory"* (Plötz, 1981, p. 168). In his view, the socialist education system is superior to its capitalist counterparts, offering *"scientific education in the true sense, which is, of course, dialectical materialistic education."* By contrast, he claims that West German students are taught *"demagogic and emotionally coloured theories and postulates"* rather than *"objective historical facts,"* with the aim *"not to develop independent judgment, but a basic anti-communist stance"* (Plötz, 1981, p. 175–176).

In the educational discourse, criticism is also directed at leftist educational thinkers in capitalist countries for their neglect of schools as spaces of communist indoctrination. Hodinka's review of Georges Snyders's "École, classe et lutte des classes" summarises Snyders's assessment of Baudelot, Estable, Bourdieu, Passeron, and Illich. These authors foster a sense of hopelessness and passivity, denying the agency of proletarian children and parents by claiming that French schools are so deeply entrenched in bourgeois ideology that striving for socialist democracy within the current system is neither possible nor necessary prior to a regime-changing revolution. Snyders, praised as *"a very smart, wide visionary, militant Marxist spirit"* (Hodinka, 1979, p. 445) contrasts the the thinkers above with Lenin: *"It took the brilliant mind of Lenin to understand that school was not to be condemned to death as a whole, but to be transformed into a means and a place for the training of the proletariat"* (Hodinka, 1979, p. 447).

Interestingly, despite their criticism of the French thinkers, Szebenyi (1977) and Plötz (1981) express similar sentiments regarding English and Western German schooling: *"Even today, the main – albeit hidden – aim of the public education policy of capitalist countries is to maintain and constantly reinforce the class structure that was established at that time. The various theories of talent and socialisation merely serve to obscure this reactionary public education policy*" (Plötz, 1981, p. 168); "*The ideals and moral values of true class struggle, which are genuinely conducive to social progress, are not to be found in England in the context of organised schooling*" (Szebenyi, 1977, p. 277).

The consensus between Szebenyi, Plötz, and Snyders is that contemporary capitalist systems and their schools represent a lower stage of historical development, one which has already been surpassed by socialist systems.

Criticism of "Western Marxism"

The criticism and rejection of Western Marxism as a version of Marxist thought is on the result of unchallengeable faith in Marxism-Leninism: "*One of the main conditions for the unity of the world communist movement is that it must be based on Marxism-Leninism as a single, integral internationalist doctrine*" (Illés, 1970, p. 34–35).

Movements and thinkers in other countries that are Marxist "in name only" (Illés, 1977, p. 357) are the main targets of this criticism: notable among these are the Frankfurt School (particularly Herbert Marcuse), Mao Zedong, Jean-Paul Sartre, and Rudi Dutschke.

The primary critique is that Western neo-Marxists regard the "young middle-class intelligentsia" (i.e. students) and "ghetto populations" along with the "Lumpenproletariat" (cf. Marcuse, 1969, p. 39) as revolutionary agents rather than a stable, organised working class: "*Marxism-Leninism rejects the false theory put forward by the radical theories of the Western left, headed by Herbert Marcuse, a professor at the University of California—that today the revolution of the young is replacing the proletarian revolution, but does not deny that student youth has an important role to play in the social struggles of the present*" (Soós, 1971).[4]

Maoism, on the other hand, deviates from Leninism in the sense that it does not aim for the education of the masses or the assimilation of cultural values from the past, nor does it draw upon the experiences of socialist countries – "*the Cultural Revolution, Lenin taught* [...] *cannot be carried out in a single leap, by force or pressure*" (Illés, 1970).

4 Cf.: "Objectively, 'in-itself,' labor still is the potentially revolutionary class; subjectively, 'for-itself,' it is not. [...] In the advanced capitalist countries, the radicalization of the working classes is counteracted by a socially engineered arrest of consciousness, and by the development and satisfaction of needs which perpetuate the servitude of the exploited" (Marcuse, 1969, p. 17).

The authors also find these trends alarming from an educational standpoint. They argue that many Western youth are misled by these ideas, hindering their ability to learn and understand the true principles of communism.

The Italian Communist thinker, Antonio Gramsci, despite being listed as a Western Marxist in the "A Dictionary of Marxist Thought" (Bottomore, 2001, p. 581), is regarded as a positive example. Today, Gramsci's legacy is subject to varied interpretations; both the New Left after 1968 and the present-day Hungarian Right are accused of misinterpreting and "appropriating" his oeuvre (Éber, 2023). However, the authors we examined consistently view him as a continuation of the work of Marx and Lenin, considering him as one of the most significant Western exponents of communism.

Criticism of radical left-wing movements in the West resulted in the exclusion of today's highly influential ideologies and policies[5] from Hungarian educational and scientific discourses. This rejection and the experiences under existing socialism is likely to have a lasting impact on the reception of similar initiatives.

Conclusions

Drawing on Gentile's original framework and the aspects of the sacralisation of politics, our research found that all four aspects (ideological superiority; moral monopoly, a utopian view of the past, present, and future; and a "sacred history") were present in the analysed sample, albeit in varying degree across different genres and topics. Performative writings, such as commemorations of historical events and personalities, personal opinions, and even obituaries used more ideologically charged terminology compared to scientific texts. Yet, even scientific discourses could not completely set aside Marxist-Leninist ideology as a reference and/or theoretic framework. Other theories and ideologies were criticised – even Marxist ones, as exampled by the rejection of Western Marxism. Further research could outline which specific topics within scientific discourses were most influenced by ideology. Additionally, it is beyond the aim and scope of this paper to analyse the timeline of political religion's presence in the journal, and scientific papers in particular, and how – and in a socio-political context: why – it changed over the observed periods.

5 As exampled by the 2022 UNESCO expert initiative for the 2030 Agenda: "Knowledge-driven actions: transforming higher education for global sustainability" in which the description of the Initiative starts with a reference to Marcuse) https://unesdoc.unesco.org/ark:/48223/pf0000380519/

Bibliography

Arendt, H. (1951). *The origins of totalitarianism*. Schocken.

Barry, G. (2015). Political religion: A user's guide. *Contemporary European History*, *24*(4), 623–638. https://doi.org/10.1017/S0960777315000375

Bhatia, V. (1993). *Analyzing genre: Language use in professional settings*. Longman.

Berger, P. L., & Luckmann, T. (1966). *The social construction of reality. A treatise in the sociology of knowledge.* Penguin Books.

Bourke, R. (2020). Political and religious ideas during the Irish revolution. *History of European Ideas*, *46*(7), 997–1008. https://doi.org/10.1080/01916599.2020.1747227

Cheruvallil-Contractor, S. (2023). When political religion is a 'good thing'? Feminist storytelling around less-heard understanding of 'political religion'. In Haynes, J. (Ed.). *Routledge handbook of religion and politics* (pp. 385–395). Routledge. https://doi.org/10.4324/9781003247265-31

Creswell, J. W. (2014). *Research design: qualitative, quantitative, and mixed methods approaches* (4th ed.). SAGE Publications.

Éder, M. Á. (2023). Antonio Gramsci második kirablása: Az antikapitalizmus egyik klasszikusának újbaloldali és újjobboldali (félre)értelmezéseiről. *Eszmélet*, *35*(138), 65–88. https://epa.oszk.hu/01700/01739/00121/pdf/EPA01739_eszmelet_138_065-088.pdf

Friedrich, C. J., & Brzezinski, Z. K. (1956). *Totalitarian dictatorship and autocracy.* Harvard University Press.

Gabriel, I. G. (2023). Political Religion: Transformation of a political concept and its ethical consequences. In Ch. Danz & J. H. Deibl (Eds.). *Transformation of religion: interdisciplinary perspectives* (pp. 163–180). Brill Schöningh. https://doi.org/10.30965/9783657790258_011

Gentile, E. (2006). *Politics as religion*. Princeton University Press.

Ignatow, G., & Mihalcea, R. (2018). *An introduction to text mining: Research design, data collection, and analysis*. SAGE Publications.

Iso-Ahola, S. (2009). The flagship journal and its role in advancing new knowledge and the field of inquiry. *Journal of Leisure Research*, *41*(3), 301–305. https://doi.org/10.1080/00222216.2009.11950174

Kestere, I., & Stonkuviene, I. (2020). From national to global? Research on the history of education in the Baltic states (1990–2015): Examining doctoral theses. *Histoire de l'éducation*, 154, 75–91. https://doi.org/10.4000/histoire-education.5575

Landwehr, A. (2008). *Historische diskursanalyse* (2nd ed.). Campus Verlag.

Maier, H. (2004, Ed.). *Totalitarianism and political religions, I: Concepts for the comparison of dictatorships.* Routledge. https://doi.org/10.4324/9780203340288

Maier, H. (2006). Political religion: A concept and its limitations. *Totalitarian Movements and Political Religions, 8*(1), 5–16. https://doi.org/10.1080/14690760601121614

Maier, H. (Ed.). (2007). *Totalitarianism and political religions, III: Theory and history of interpretations.* Routledge. https://doi.org/10.4324/9780203942451

Maier, H., & Schäfer, M. (Ed.). (2007). *Totalitarianism and political religions, II: Concepts for the comparison of dictatorships.* Routledge. https://doi.org/10.4324/9780203935422

Morgan, J. W. (2005). Marxism and moral education. *Journal of Moral Education, 34*(4), 391–398. https://doi.org/10.1080/03057240500410079

Nyirkos, T. (2023). Patriotism as a political religion: Its history, its ambiguities, and the case of hungary. *Religions, 14*(1), 116. https://doi.org/10.3390/rel14010116

Payne, S. G. (2005). On the heuristic value of the concept of political religion and its application. *Totalitarian Movements and Political Religions, 6*(2), 163–174. https://doi.org/10.1080/14690760500181537

Polyák, Zs., Somogyvári, L., & Németh, A. (2021). Iskolai énektanítás és kórusmozgalom a politikai vallás terjesztésének szolgálatában – egy lehetséges értelmezési keret felvázolása. In Á. Engler, & V. Bocsi (Eds.), *Új kutatások a neveléstudományokban, 2020* [New Researches in the Education Sciences, 2020] (pp. 229–244.). Magyar Tudományos Akadémia Pedagógiai Tudományos Bizottság. http://onk.hu/2020/downloads/Uj_kutatasok_a_nevelestudomanyban_2020_02.pdf

Polyák, Zs., Szabó, Z. A., & Németh, A. (2021). The political religion of communism in Hungarian children's choir compositions between 1958–1989. *Historia Scholastica, 7*(1), 85–109. https://doi.org/10.15240/tul/006/2021-1-005

Richards, D. A. J. (2023). Patriarchal religion in US constitutional law (*Dobbs* v. *Jackson*): Originalism as "political religion" (Burke) unmasked. *Contemporary Psychoanalysis, 59*(1–2), 23–42. https://doi.org/10.1080/00107530.2023.2239683

Somogyvári, L., Polyák, Zs., & Németh, A. (2021). Új elméleti keretek a szocialista neveléstudomány vizsgálatára: A politikai vallás. *Magyar Pedagógia, 121*(1), 85–97. https://doi.org/10.17670/mped.2021.1.85

Somogyvári, L., & Polyák, Zs. (2022). A „tudományos-technikai forradalom" diskurzusai a magyar neveléstudományban. *Múltunk, 67*(3). 111–131. https://doi.org/10.56944/multunk.2022.3.4

Somogyvári, L., & Polyák, Zs. (2023). A számítógép és a tudományos-technikai forradalom a pedagógiai diskurzusokban (1968–1977): szerzői és intézményi hátterek. In Zs. Molnár-Kovács, H. Andl & J. Steklács (Eds.). *Új kutatások a neveléstudományokban, 2022* (pp. 48–57). Magyar Tudományos Akadémia Pedagógiai Tudományos Bizottság. https://konferencia.pte.hu/sites/konferencia.pte.hu/files/UKN_2022.pdf

Voegelin, E. (1999). The political religions. In M. Hennigsen (Ed.), *Modernity without restraint* (Vol. 5, pp. 19–74). University of Missouri Press.

Analysed papers

Bodó, L. (1971). Szabolcs Ottó: Szocialista hazafiságra és proletár nemzetköziségre nevelés a történelemtanításban. *Magyar Pedagógia, 71*(3), 352–353.

Bólyai, I. (1972). A marxista nevelés története – olasz szerzőtől. *Magyar Pedagógia, 72*(1), 81–84.

Földes, É. (1972). Kommunista tudós a francia Panthéonban. *Magyar Pedagógia, 72*(3), 358–363.

Földes É. (1977). Utópia és realizmus a mindenoldalú harmonikus személyiségfejlesztéssel kapcsolatos elképzelésekben. *Magyar Pedagógia, 77*(3–4), 355–358.

Gáspár, L. (1973). Manacorda, M. A.: Marx és a mai pedagógia. *Magyar Pedagógia, 73*(1–2), 223–225.

Gáspár, L. (1983). A marxizmus reneszánsza és a neveléstudomány. *Magyar Pedagógia, 83*(3), 223–233.

Hodinka, L. (1979). Georges Snyders: École classe et lutte des classes. *Magyar Pedagógia, 79*(4), 445–447.

Illés, L. (1970). Lenin, a kulturális forradalom és korunk. *Magyar Pedagógia, 70*(1), 26–41.

Mészáros, I. (1969). Emlékülések a Magyar Tudományos Akadémián. *Magyar Pedagógia, 69*(1–2), 183–187.

Plötz, R. (1981). Szocialista és monopolkapitalista neveléspolitika az NDK, NSZK és Nyugat-Berlin tanterveinek tükrében. *Magyar Pedagógia, 81*(2), 168–178.

Simon, Gy. (1973). Az iskolák államosításának történelmi jelentősége Magyarországon. *Magyar Pedagógia, 73*(4), 399–405.

Simon, Gy. (1980). Köte Sándor: A Tanácsköztársaság közoktatáspolitikai és pedagógiai törekvései. *Magyar Pedagógia, 80*(1), 102–104.

Soós, P. (1971). Hermann István: A szocialista kultúra problémái. *Magyar Pedagógia*, *71*(1–2), 180–182.

Szebenyi, P. (1973). Hazai törekvések a laikus erkölcstan iskolai bevezetésére. *Magyar Pedagógia*, *73*(1–2), 132–144.

Szebenyi, P. (1977). A morális értékrendszer közvetítésének problémái Angliában a szervezett oktatás keretei között. *Magyar Pedagógia*, *77*(2), 271–277.

Tőkéczki, L. (1985). Az egyházak és az iskoláztatás Klebelsberg Kunó nézeteiben. *Magyar Pedagógia*, *85*(1), 69–78.

Trencsényi, L. (1989). Krupszkaja-reneszánsz és a közoktatás peresztrojkája. *Magyar Pedagógia*, *89*(2), 188–191.

Tibor Darvai[1]

Educational psychology and scientific recruitment: Candidates and academic doctors at the intersection of educational science and psychology in 1950s–1960s Hungary

Abstract: In 1956, due to Khrushchev's policy of de-Stalinisation, the discrediting of psychology was abolished throughout the socialist bloc. From then on, unlike in the Stalinist era, it became possible to legitimately pursue studies in psychology and obtain a scientific degree in the discipline. This was also true for educational psychology, which was situated at the intersection of education sciences and psychology. In Hungary, in the late 1950s, those who obtained a candidate title in educational psychology did so in the field of education sciences. However, by the end of the 1960s, educational psychology had become detached from education sciences and had shifted to the field of psychology. As such, academic doctorates in educational psychology are now awarded in the field of psychology rather than education sciences. One consequence of this change was that scientific recruitment in educational psychology no longer contributed to the enrichment of education sciences, but to that of psychology. The present research outlines the history of this change.

Keywords: scientific recruitment, educational science, psychology, socialism, Kádár era

Introduction: Politics, education, and psychology in 1950s–1960s Hungary

By the end of the 1940s, as in all East-Central European states, the Communist Party had seised political power in Hungary, transforming it into a one-party, Soviet-style Stalinist dictatorship. By 1950, the Stalinist regime-building process had reached the fields of science, education sciences, and public education.[2]

---

1 Bárczi Gusztáv Faculty of Special Needs Education, ELTE Eötvös Loránd University, Budapest, Hungary, darvai.tibor@barczi.elte.hu

2 In this study, Stalinism is characterised as an anti-capitalist ideology and political practice, the central elements of which are, on the one hand, include forced industrialisation, colonialism, state terror, a planned economy, and the cult of the leader. On the other hand, as an anti-capitalist ideology, it was formulated in opposition to capitalism, and therefore included the reduction of social inequalities and the promotion of social justice among its core aims, which it sought to achieve through the aforementioned means (Fitzpatrick, 2000; Kotkin, 1995).

Following the Soviet Stalinist science policy, the 1950 resolution of the Hungarian Working People's Party discredited scientific trends and institutions of Western origin in Hungary (Kardos & Kornidesz, 1990), as was the case in all Soviet-influenced countries at the time. Fields such as genetics, psychology, sociology, and pedology, among others, were among those that were discredited (Golnhofer & Szabolcs, 2013; Knausz 1986; Sáska, 2005, 2008, 2011, 2017).

The 1950 party resolution on educational policy held the National Educational Scientific Institute,[3] headed by Ferenc Mérei,[4] responsible for the mistakes made in public education. Established in 1948, a pivotal year, the Institute was tasked with replicating the Soviet Stalinist model and establishing a Soviet-style public education system in Hungary. However, what was legitimate in 1948 had become unacceptable by 1950, as the process of Stalinisation, which did not tolerate alternatives, had extended into public education and science. The 1950 educational party resolution also accused the National Educational Scientific Institute of promoting bourgeois Western ideologies, disrupting textbook publishing, and contributing to the high drop-out rate among children of working-class origin. As a result, the institute was dissolved, and its staff were stigmatised as anti-Marxists, the cardinal sin of the era (Lázár, 1950; Péter, 1954; Sáska, 2008).

The educational policy decision highlights the way in which the Stalinist establishment of the early 1950s marginalised the child-centred pedagogy and pedology that had been the main pedagogical approach in the Soviet Union before Stalin, and advocated for by Mérei. This anti-pedology stance echoed the Stalinist ideology of the early 1930s: the idea of the autonomous child as articulated by psychology was not compatible with the Stalinist state's top-down control, which did not tolerate autonomy or alternative perspectives. Consequently, the child-centred school was replaced by a state-centred socialist pedagogy (Sáska, 2015b). As a result, pedagogy took the place of pedology, and psychology ceased to exist as an

3 The National Educational Scientific Institute was established in 1948 as the successor to the National Council of Public Education. Its primary task was to organise a Soviet-style public education system. It was abolished in 1950 following a Stalinist educational party decision. The party resolution branded the institute as a "hotbed of bourgeois educational science" and its director Ferenc Mérei as a "bourgeois deviant".

4 Ferenc Mérei (1909–1986) was a psychologist and educational scientist who remained a socialist-communist until his death. His scientific work explored aspects of the social determination of the individual, exemplified by his research on "togetherness" (Mérei, 1969). He also contributed to child psychology, experimental psychology, and clinical psychology. He was imprisoned until 1963 due to his involvement in the 1956 revolution.

independent discipline. Psychology was integrated into medical science, merged with Pavlovian physiology with its natural scientific objectivity, and subordinated to pedagogical logic.

The education policy decision achieved its goals and redefined the field of education sciences. The newly established educational scientific elite, now holding a monopoly, developed a socialist pedagogy closely aligned with the party's demands (Golnhofer & Szabolcs, 2013; Knausz, 1994; Mihály, 1999; Sáska, 2015a). Didactics emerged as perhaps the most important sub-discipline within the new education sciences (Sáska, 2009). This shift meant that every aspect of the teaching-learning process was determined by pedagogical rather than psychological considerations. Consequently, the writing and editing of textbooks, as well as aspects of further training and supervision – at least formally – followed this approach.

Psychology and pedology were disempowered in the Stalinist era, so it is not surprising that the end of their marginalisation can be dated to the post-Stalinist era, beginning in 1956. In his speech at the 20th Congress of the USSR Communist Party, Khrushchev proclaimed an anti-Stalinist policy, or in other words, de-Stalinisation.[5]

In line with Khrushchev's new policy, the de-Stalinisation of pedagogy and education began in the Soviet Union. A clear indication of this shift was the publication in the 1956 issue of the Soviet journal *Pedagogika* of a paper entitled "Study the child in multiple ways and in thorough detail!".[6] The article argued that it is necessary to examine the age-specific characteristics of children within a Marxist framework, cleansed of Stalinist elements, and called for a reflection on the psychological development of the human being (N. A., 1957). The Soviet socialist educational theory underwent a half-turn. While it endorsed the 1936 decision of the USSR Central Committee to abolish pedology, it also partially rehabilitated the study of the child and a reinterpreted, non-bourgeois version of Marxist psychology (Sáska, 2008).

De-Stalinisation also meant the end of the discrediting of psychology, which had been sidelined for almost a decade. As ideology and science policy softened,

5 De-Stalinisation is defined as a counterpoint to Stalinist policy, yet remains rooted in anti-capitalist ideology and political practice. However, unlike Stalinism, the socialist-communist party does not seek total control of society. It allows for alternatives in all areas of social life, albeit with exclusively socialist content. Furthermore, the emphasis on the material well-being of the individual is viewed as an important element of politics (Jones, 2006).

6 This article from *Sovietskaya Pedagogika* was published in Hungarian translation in the first issue of *Pedagogical Review* in 1957. This translation is referenced throughout the rest of the paper.

psychology began to be re-institutionalised. In 1957, the Psychology Committee was established within the Hungarian Academy of Sciences. The emancipation of psychology from educational science and their gradual institutional separation were evidenced by the simultaneous launch of two annual book series, *Psychological Studies* and *Studies from the Circle of Education Sciences*, by the Academy Publishing House in 1958. *The Hungarian Psychological Review*, which had been discontinued in the early 1950s, was relaunched in 1960, and *Hungarian Pedagogy*, also discontinued in the early 1950s, was relaunched a year later in 1961.[7] This synchronicity cannot be a mere coincidence.

The increasing autonomy of psychology is evidenced by the foundation of the Hungarian Psychological Scientific Society (MPTT) in 1962. In 1963, the independent training of psychologists had already begun at Eötvös Loránd University (Kovai, 2016). With its institutionalisation, the discipline of psychology sought to distance itself from the then-disintegrated Marxist philosophy. It aimed to collaborate with yet differentiate itself from pedagogy and gently separate from psychiatry, which remained a part of the medical field (Pléh, 1998, 2016).

From the perspective of scientific recruitment, after 1956, it became possible to obtain scientific titles, candidacy, and academic doctorate degrees in educational psychology, which is at the intersection of educational science and psychology. In socialist science, these two scientific degrees were known by the terms "candidate" and "Doctor of Science", the latter sometimes referred to as "academic doctor". In the late 1950s and early 1960s, acquiring these degrees first became possible in the field of education sciences. However, from the second half of the 1960s, candidate degrees in educational psychology were no longer awarded in the field of education sciences, but in psychology. The research below outlines the history of this change.

The interpretative framework, questions, and sources of research

Unlike the pre-1948–1949 system, but following the Soviet model, universities lost the right to award scientific degrees in 1950. From then on, only the Hungarian Academy of Sciences was entitled to confer scientific degrees, a task carried out by the newly established Scientific Qualification Committee (TMB) within the Academy. These changes also resulted in the university system losing much of its autonomy. From that point, it was not the universities but a "superior" institution that awarded doctorate titles.

At the same time, the Soviet-style aspirant model was introduced, contrasting with the Western-style PhD training. At the end of the aspirant term, candidates

7 On the abolition of Hungarian Pedagogy in 1950, see the study by Pénzes (2016).

defended their scientific dissertations in a public debate and were subsequently awarded the title of candidacy.[8] In Soviet-style scientific systems, the next scientific degree was the Doctor of Science, which required a candidate's degree. The title of Doctor of Science was equivalent to that of a professor.[9]

The number of candidates and academic doctors also served as an indicator of a discipline's importance and its degree of institutionalisation (Brezsnyánszky, 2015; Karády, 2015; Pénzes, 2013; Sáska, 2016). The more candidates and academic doctors a science had, the more important it became. At the same time, the number of individuals holding a candidate title was also a key aspect of scientific recruitment, and therefore had a major impact on the future of the discipline.

The present research investigates changes in the number of candidates and academic doctors specialising in educational psychology during the 1960s. Applying this framework, the study analyses candidates and academic doctors within the field of education sciences working in psychology, as well as those within the field of psychology specialising in pedagogy. In this context, we examined the following questions:

1. What was the background of the educational psychologists? In other words, from which professional fields were educational psychologists recruited?
2. How did the number of individuals holding candidate and academic doctorate titles in the field of educational psychology change during the 1960s?
3. Where did these individuals obtain their candidate or academic doctorate titles? In Hungary or in the Soviet Union?
4. What types of workplaces employed educational psychology researchers?
5. Did educational psychology predominantly align with educational science or psychology in the 1960s? Has this changed over time?
6. How have these factors influenced the issue of scientific recruitment?

These issues are also relevant to the aspect of scientific recruitment, since it is crucial to distinguish whether educational psychology reinforces educational science or psychology. If educational psychology is part of education sciences, then it primarily trains scientists for that field, but if it is part of psychology, then it trains researchers in psychology.

To answer the research questions, this study examines the Academic Almanachs (Almanach, 1962, 1967, 1970, 1973) and the Reports of the Hungarian Academy of Sciences (Akadémiai Értesítő, 1952–1972). Additionally, the Pedagogical Lexicons (Báthory & Falus, 1997; Nagy, 1976–1979) are used to investigate biographical

8 The candidate's degree was the Soviet equivalent of the Western-style PhD.

9 The research will henceforth use the term "academic doctor".

elements. The Academic Almanac and the Academic Reports are considered to be official publications of the Hungarian Academy of Sciences, are authorised by the Academy, and are considered reliable sources documenting the state of socialist science.

Disciplinary classifications in the socialist era were fluid and subject to change. Therefore, our analysis did not solely rely on disciplinary categorisation, but also drew heavily on the direction and field of the researchers' scientific work. For example, an individual academically classified as having a degree in another field of psychology or education sciences, such as educational theory, work psychology, or general psychology, could still be considered a researcher in educational psychology if their research and publications indicated that the individual was a specialist in that field. It is important to note that before 1956, it was not possible to get a degree in psychology at all, only in educational science. The prohibition from the Stalinist era was lifted by the process of de-Stalinisation that began in 1956, which subsequently made it possible to obtain scientific degrees in psychology as well as educational psychology, as mentioned earlier.

Candidates and academic doctors at the intersections of education sciences and psychology in the 1960s

According to the Academic Almanac published in 1962, there were 18 candidates in education sciences (Almanac, 1962). Of this professional-scientific community, six researchers—that is, one-third of those who received a candidate's degree—can be classified as educational psychologists (see Table 1).

Education scientists working on psychology can be divided into two groups. The first includes those who were active in the field of psychology before Stalinism initiated marginalisation. The second group consists of those who began working in psychology after 1956, after the end of its discreditation. Among these "old ones" were Dezső Hildebrand Várkonyi[10] and Erzsébet Baranyai.[11] From 1929, Várkonyi headed the independent Pedagogical-Psychology Institute at the University of Szeged, focusing on child studies and educational psychology (Pukánszky, 2021). In 1952 he was awarded his candidate's degree based on his work rather than the defence of his candidate's thesis. This was possible in the early years of the emerging Soviet-style scientific system, which required older,

10 Dezső Várkonyi's (1888–1971), originally named Dezső Hildebrand Várkonyi, was a Benedictine priest-teacher. After the communist takeover in 1948, he dropped the name "Hildebrand" due to its Catholic origins.

11 Erzsébet Baranyai (1894–1976) was a researcher of educational psychology and an apprentice of Dezső Várkonyi.

scientifically qualified individuals to participate in the candidate defences of the young scholars and judge their candidate dissertations. Várkonyi's apprentice, Erzsébet Baranyi, a former Montessori committed educationalist, can also be placed in this first group (Báthory & Falus, 1997; Nagy, 1976–1979). However, by 1962 they had both reached retirement age and were no longer active researchers.

Among the new candidates in educational psychology, it is noteworthy that a significant number of them did not obtain their candidate titles in Hungary, but in the Soviet Union. Among these researchers were Lajos Bartha, Lajos Duró, and Jenő Salamon. Lajos Duró was an aspirant at the Herzen Pedagogical College in Leningrad between 1953 and 1957, as was Lajos Bartha between 1955 and 1958 (Nagy, 1976–1979).[12] It was only those who had studied psychology in the Soviet Union – and thus had no contact with Western schools of psychology, which were stigmatised as bourgeois – were allowed to practice educational psychology with the approval of the Party. The professional and ideological socialisation milieu within the Soviet Union also influenced researchers' reputations. Being socialised in the USSR rendered scientists unquestionably loyal to the socialist system.

Only László Kelemen deviated from this pattern, as he had earned his candidate's degree in Hungary. The scientific degrees obtained in the Soviet Union were particularly important, especially considering the relationship between educational psychology and psychology. Moreover, the dissertation titles of researchers who received their candidate degrees in the Soviet Union tended to be predominantly ideological.

The relationship between the old and the new educational psychology researchers is exemplified by Erzsébet Baranyai's study entitled "The Development of Logical Thinking in the Context of Teaching Arithmetic and Grammar", published in the first issue of *Pedagogical Review* (Lénárd-Baranyai, 1951). This article sparked a serious debate in both *Public Education* and *Pedagogical Review* (Kardos, 1952; Kerékgyártó, 1952; Lénárd-Baranyai, 1952; N. A., 1952).[13] Following the debate, the editorial board of the *Pedagogical Review* acknowledged

---

12 Lajos Bartha was a professional soldier between 1948 and 1959. In the late 1950s, he left the military to pursue a career in science. Between 1957 and 1959 he was a lecturer at the Pedagogical-Psychological Department of the Moscow Political Military Academy.

13 The journals *Pedagogical Review* and *Public Education* were two of the most influential pedagogical journals of the period. *Pedagogical Review* catered primarily to educational researchers, while *Public Education* was geared more toward educationalists. In accordance with the Stalinist approach of opposing alternative viewpoints, *Pedagogical Review* was the only educational scientific journal of the period. It served as the periodical of the Ministry of Education until 1954 and was published by the Pedagogical Institute of Science from 1955.

errors that were made in the interpretation of Baranyai's research, such as the usage of civic psychology terminology. The board defended the authors, stating "we do not agree with those critics who see the authors as the enemy" (N. A., 1952, p. 568). It is also possible that the editors of the *Pedagogical Review* supported Erzsébet Baranyai because the scientific qualification system required her expertise at that time.[14]

Looking at the jobs they held, it is clear that the three researchers in educational psychology who obtained their candidate titles in the Soviet Union worked at the Pedagogical Institute of Science in the late 1950s.[15] Thus, the Pedagogical Scientific Institute can be regarded as the scientific institute from which the "backbone" of the new educational psychology team emerged. These developments suggest that, although practicing psychology and educational psychology was legitimised after 1956, there was a need for educational psychology researchers whose professional-scientific and ideological views were beyond reproach in the new socialist system. This might have occurred with the approval of the ruling Hungarian Workers' Party, given that Hungary remained a one-party dictatorship until 1989/1990.

Table 1: Candidates in educational science specialising in psychology in 1962 (own editing)

Name	Date of birth	Year/place of degree obtained	Dissertation title	Scientific area	Workplace
Erzsébet Baranyai	1894	1956	Logical relation of meanings in expressions, conjunctions in composition	educational psychology	1949–1962: MTA Psychological Institute, senior research fellow; 1963: retired

14 In 1952 the editorial board of the Pedagogical Review included György Ágoston, István Szokolszky, and Béla Tettamanti, as well as Magda Jóború, the Deputy Minister of Education.

15 The Pedagogical Scientific Institute was established in 1954 and was tasked with managing public education. It was also responsible for developing curricula, textbooks, and training courses. In addition, the institute produced scientific work. From 1955, the *Pedagogical Review* was the institute's journal.

Name	Date of birth	Year/place of degree obtained	Dissertation title	Scientific area	Workplace
Lajos Bartha	1927	1959 Soviet Union	Education for professional engagement in military officer schools	developmental psychology	1959–1961: staff member of the Pedagogical Scientific Institute (PTI); 1960–1962: Associate Professor, Department of Psychology, ELTE; 1962: Director of the of Psychology Institute of the Hungarian Academy of Sciences
Lajos Duró	1928	1957 Soviet Union	The education of proletarian nationality in the educational process (based on the teaching of history) in the upper classes of Soviet and Hungarian schools	general psychology	1957–1958: Ministry of Education, Department of Secondary Education – Lecturer; 1958–1961: PTI Department of Educational Theory – research associate; 1960–1970: Associate Professor, Department of Educational Science and Psychology, University of Szeged; 1970–1990: Head of the independent Department of Psychology at the same institution

(Continued)

Table 1: (Continued)

Name	Date of birth	Year/place of degree obtained	Dissertation title	Scientific area	Workplace
László Kelemen	1919	1957	Concepts and thinking in lower primary school	educational psychology	1948: lecturer and head of the Department of Education at the Teacher Training College of Pécs; 1964–1966: Head of the independent Department of Psychology; 1966–1981: Founder and Head of the Department of Educational Science and later of the Department of Psychology at the University of Debrecen
Jenő Salamon	1930	1958 Soviet Union (Moscow)	Age specificity of elementary constructive activity of schoolchildren (first, third, fifth grades)	development psychology	1958–1961: staff member of the PTI, 1961–: Head of the Department of Psychology, ELTE; 1973–: Head of the Department of Developmental and Educational Psychology at ELTE
Dezső Várkonyi	1888	1952	[note: for a life's work and not for defence]	pedagogical psychology	1954: retirement

The relationship between educational science and psychology is highlighted by the fact that in 1962, Lajos Kardos,[16] who worked in the field of general psychology, was awarded an academic doctorate in education sciences, not psychology (Table 2).[17] This can be seen as an indication of the supremacy of educational science over psychology, a holdover from the Stalinist era that persisted into the early Kádár era. It also shows that despite the rehabilitation of psychology in the late 1950s, its re-institutionalisation and acceptance were gradual, and the discipline continued to face stigmatisation. It is important to remember that the practice of psychology in the socialist-era was viewed as a Western-oriented, "bourgeois science", which positioned its practitioners as figures of opposition. In addition this, psychology's self-perception included a sense of "being in the minority"; in the early 1960s, only about a dozen people were working in the field (Pléh, 1998).

In the 1950s, Lajos Kardos was the sole representative of psychology to the "authorities" and thus played a major role in maintaining the continuity of the discipline. According to the Stalinist model, psychology had to be subjected to either pedagogy or Pavlovian physiology (Joravsky, 1989; Pléh, 2010). Kardos, with a medical degree, opted for the Pavlovian approach over pedagogy for two main reasons. First, from a professional perspective, it was easier to transfer medical-psychological knowledge to physiology. The second reason was more ideological: pedagogy in Soviet-style systems was always subject to the ideology of the state - hence its socialist characterisation - whereas physiology did not involve the same level of ideological interference. This logic also appeared in Kardos' academic thesis linking Pavlov's research to psychology, where he wrote the following: "To do this work [to validate the results of Pavlov's research in psychology –comment of T. D.] in the whole of psychology, in full depth and in a complete system: this is the aim of this dissertation" (Kardos, 1955, p. 546). Regarding Lajos Kardos' relationship with Pavlovian research, one of Kardos' apprentices noted that in Kardos' eyes, his Pavlovian research was more of a survival strategy than full identification. Indeed, Kardos directed the new generation of scientists towards behaviourism and Gestalt psychology (Hunyady, 1996). Another apprentice of Kardos, confirming this line of thought, argued that Kardos

16 Lajos Kardos (1889–1985) studied at the University of Vienna - due to the numerus clausus - where he obtained a medical degree. Here, as an apprentice of Karl Bühler, he became acquainted with Gestalt psychology. He then moved to America, where he became involved with behaviourism. Upon returning home, he studied under Lipót Szondi, adopting the analytical approach (Hunyady, 1996).

17 In 1962, along with Lajos Kardos, the didacticist Sándor Nagy was the other academic doctor in the field of educational science (Almanac, 1962).

framed the results of contemporary American behaviourist research on animal learning in a Pavlovian framework (Pléh, 2016). Overall, it can be claimed that Kardos was a central figure in the re-institutionalising psychology, representing Western psychology, including American psychology. In the 1950s, he played a major role in transmitting psychological knowledge, and can be seen as a founding father psychologist training at ELTE in the early 1960s, where he was head of the department.

Table 2: Academic doctors in educational science specialising in psychology in 1962 (own editing)

Name	Date of birth	Year/place of degree obtained	Dissertation title	Scientific area	Workplace
Lajos Kardos	1899	1955	Pavlov's research and psychology	general psychology	1963–1971: Head of the Department of Psychology, ELTE

The initial phase of the re-institutionalisation of psychology after 1956 is underscored by the fact that, in 1962, there were only four candidates in the field of psychology (Ferenc Hepp, György Geréb, Ferenc Lénárd, and Zsolt Tánczos) compared to 18 candidates in education sciences. The 1962 Academic Almanac does not indicate the specific fields in which these psychology candidates obtained their degrees, so one has to rely on the 1967 Almanac.[18] According to the 1967 Almanac, Ferenc Hepp was the only person with a candidate title in educational psychology. However, based on his publications, his field of specialisation was more in the field of sports psychology and basketball methodology (Nagy, 1977, p. 128). As a specialist in educational psychology, György Geréb can also be considered. After initially completing his candidate's degree in educational science, he later transferred to psychology. In his case, the pedagogical line is further evidenced from his teaching role at the Department of Education Sciences of the Szeged Teacher Training College. Although Ferenc Lénárd was categorised as a specialist in general psychology, his main research area was problem-solving thinking in primary schools, placing him in the field of pedagogy (Báthory & Falus, 1997; Nagy, 1976–1979). In this way, Lénárd can also be classified as a psychologist working in the field of pedagogy.

18 According to the 1967 Almanac, Ferenc Hepp received his candidate's degree in educational psychology, while György Geréb specialised in work psychology. Ferenc Lénárd and Zsolt Tánczos researched general psychology.

Examining the workplace, György Geréb was affiliated with a college, a pattern also observed in the case of László Kelemen mentioned earlier. In the 1950s, Ferenc Lénárd worked at the Pedagogical Scientific Institute, as did the researchers in educational psychology mentioned above (Lajos Bartha, Lajos Duró, and Jenő Salamon). From the early 1960s, Lénárd worked at the Psychological Institute of the Hungarian Academy of Sciences, headed by Lajos Bartha, with whom he had previously been acquainted.

Table 3: Candidates in psychology specialising in pedagogy in 1962 (own editing)

Name	Date of birth	Year/place of degree obtained	Dissertation title	Scientific area	Workplace
Ferenc Hepp	1909	1960	Main issues in the perception of sports movements	pedagogical psychology	1959–1969: Director of the Institute for Scientific Research in Physical Education; 1969-: Professor at the College of Physical Education
György Geréb	1923	1957	Main features of Comenius' didactic views	labour psychology	1949–1963: Szeged Teacher Training College, Department of Educational Science 1963–1982: Organizer and head at the Department of Psychology
Ferenc Lénárd	1911	1961	Problem-solving thinking	general psychology	1954–1962: PTI staff member; 1962–1972: Psychology Institute of the Hungarian Academy of Sciences

By 1970, the number of candidates in education sciences had increased to 46 from 18 in 1962 (Almanac, 1970). However, within this group, the number of candidates specialising in psychology decreased from six to three by 1970 (cf. Table 1). In fact, a closer examination of the candidates in education sciences dealing with psychology reveals that Ferenc Pataki is the only one who is clearly identifiable (see Table 4), as Dezső Várkonyi and Erzsébet Baranyai had already reached retirement age. In other words, there was a noticeable shift of psychologically-oriented researchers moving from the field of education sciences into psychology, which will be detailed in the later sections of this study.

Ferenc Pataki's professional career is also relevant as it reflects changes in the direction of the Hungarian socialist system. Before 1950, Pataki was a student at a NÉKOSZ college during the pre-Stalinist period.[19] In the early 1950s, during the Stalinist-era, he graduated from the Moscow Pedagogical College with a degree in pedagogy and psychology, and then became an aspirant at the Political College of the Hungarian Working People's Party. During the period of de-Stalinisation in 1956, he was one of the organisers of the Petőfi Circle's Pedagogical debate.[20] The new socialist regime led by János Kádár had branded the Petőfi Circle as the intellectual antecedent of the revolution. This led to interruptions in Pataki's promising career is interrupted, and he was "relegated" to the role of a primary school teacher. However, at the beginning of the 1960s, the repression ceased and a period of consolidation began. During this time several people were rehabilitated, including Pataki. In 1961, he joined the staff of the Pedagogical Scientific Institute and its successor, the National Pedagogical Institute.

In his candidate dissertation, Pataki examined Makarenko's work, interpreting him not only as an educator but also as a social psychologist who applied his knowledge of social psychology in the field of pedagogy and the organisation of children's communities (Pataki, 1968). This perspective highlights why Pataki's research included both social psychology and educational theory. From a research point of view, the classification of social psychology as a distinct sub-discipline is also relevant, as at that time it was possible to practice not only psychology but also social psychology. This is reflected in Pataki's collaboration with Ferenc Lénárd and Lajos Bartha at the Psychological Institute of the Hungarian Academy of Sciences starting in 1965.

19 The National Association of People's Colleges (NÉKOSZ) was founded in July 1946. The People's Colleges were residential institutions aimed at educating poor young people, mostly from peasant backgrounds, to become intellectuals. Initially supported by the Communist Party, it soon became a national movement, but lost support from the party after 1948 and was abolished in 1949.

20 The Petőfi Circle was founded in 1955 as a forum for young communist intellectuals. In 1956, several public debates were held in the Petőfi Circle (e.g., press debates and historian debates). In these public debates, they criticised Mátyás Rákosi and his circle, as well as the Stalinist methods of governance. Similar criticisms emerged during teachers' debates on public education and education sciences. After the suppression of the revolution, the Petőfi Circle was stigmatised as a breeding ground which had taken part in fomenting the revolution. As a result, a number of participants were convicted or dismissed from their jobs.

Table 4: Candidates of education sciences specialised in psychology in 1970 (own editing)

Name	Date of birth	Year/place of degree obtained	Dissertation title	Scientific area	Workplace
Erzsébet Baranyai	1894	1956	Logical relation of meanings in expressions, conjunctions in composition	educational psychology	1949–1962: MTA Psychological Institute, senior research fellow; 1963: retired
Dezső Várkonyi	1888	1952	[note: for a life's work and not for defence]	pedagogical psychology	1954: retirement
Ferenc Pataki	1928	1968	The life and pedagogy of Makarenko	educational theory, social psychology	1955–1961: primary school teacher; 1961–1965: adjunct professor at the PTI, then the National Pedagogical Institute and the Pedagogical Seminary of Budapest; 1965–1975: staff member of the Institute of Psychology, 1975–1993: director

By 1970, the number of candidates in psychology had risen to 24, up from just four in 1962, and the number of educational psychologists increased from three to 11 (Almanac, 1970). This indicates that almost every second candidate in psychology were working on topics related to educational psychology or pedagogy. There are two components to this growth. Firstly, individuals such as Lajos Duró and Jenő Salamon, who previously had a candidate title in educational psychology within the field of education sciences, transitioned into the field of psychology. Although this trend is not a significant in terms of numbers, it shows the direction of the change: the migration from education sciences to psychology. The other component, which is more significant from a quantitative point of view, is the entry into the field of psychology by the generation born in the late 1920s or early 1930s who obtained their candidate's degrees in the mid-1960s. For these newcomers, the presence of a college culture remained dominant. Notably, only one individual defended a candidate's dissertation in the Soviet Union, suggesting that while the Soviet connection still persisted, it was not as significant in the 1960s as it was in the late 1950s.

Although not apparent from the present table, according to the data in the academic almanacs, a significant number of the opponents evaluating the new candidates in educational psychology were researchers who had obtained their candidate titles after 1956.[21] This group includes Lajos Bartha, Lajos Duró, László Kelemen, Jenő Salamon, and Ferenc Lénárd. They are recognised as the founders of socialist-oriented educational psychology (Darvai, 2019).

The migration of educational psychology researchers from educational science to psychology has had a significant impact on scientific recruitment. In fact, the latest generation of educational psychology researchers have contributed more to psychology than to educational science. These new researchers had already been trained in educational psychology by the generation that had obtained their scientific degrees in the late 1950s and early 1960s. Consequently, psychologists who had identified themselves as such before 1956, such as Lajos Kardos, abandoned the field of educational psychology, leaving it to those who came after 1956, who are now recognised as the founders of socialist educational psychology.

Our argument seems to be supported by the history of the Psychological Institute of Eötvös Loránd University in the early 1970s. In 1970, following the retirement of Lajos Kardos, Béla Radnai was appointed as the head of the institute but passed away the same year. Subsequently, two departments were established: one for general psychology and another for developmental psychology and educational psychology. As György Hunyady wrote: *"one for western, one for eastern professional orientation, one for informal, one for formal party-state influence"* (Hunyady, 1996, p. 9). Ilona Barkóczi became the head of the Department of General Psychology, and Jenő Salamon tasked with heading the Department of Developmental Psychology. The fact that the division headed by Ilona Barkóczi was referred to as 'The Department' by psychology students hints at underlying ideological and professional conflicts (Hunyady, 1996; Pléh, 2016). The phenomenon of double or parallel departments was not exclusive to the softening Kádár-era; similar divisions could also be found at the University of Szeged in the 1920s, although the divide then East and West, but Catholic and Protestant (Fizel, 2014, 2018).

21 Károly Domján's opponents were Ferenc Lénárd and Jenő Salamon, while László Nagy's opponents were Ferenc Lénárd and Lajos Duró. One of the opponents of Edit S. Molnár was the educational psychologist Lajos Duró, along with his counterpoint, Lajos Kardos.

This recurring pattern suggests that the conflict between pedagogy and psychology is a systematic feature independent of political systems.

Looking at the workplaces of the candidates in educational psychology, it can be seen that the representatives of the new socialist educational psychology were successively integrated into the higher education and academic system. Moreover, their affiliation with the Psychological Institute of the Hungarian Academy of Sciences remained intact.

The analysis of the titles of the new candidate theses shows that the ideologically-charged topics were relegated to the background, giving way to a more professional focus on the teaching-learning process as the object of the research. However, this shift does not suggest that state socialist ideology was entirely abandoned in favour of a non-ideological professional approach. On the contrary, from the 1960s onwards, it was Marxist psychology rather than state socialist ideology that legitimised psychological research. This development was made possible by the fragmentation of state socialist ideology, a key characteristic of the Kádár regime (Rainer, 2011), which did not, or could not, fully control all aspects of social life. One aspect of this trend is also evident in the field of psychology. Various departments were granted the opportunity to define psychology within a certain framework, but on the basis of their own values, interests, and traditions.

Table 5: Candidates in psychology specialising in pedagogy in 1970 (own editing)

Name	Date of birth	Year/place of degree obtained	Dissertation title	Scientific area	Workplace
Károly Domján	1930	1965	Development and specificities of the understanding of cause and effect in lower primary school	pedagogical psychology	1952–1964: Lecturer and Deputy Director of the Department of Educational Science at the Teacher Training College of Pécs; 1964–1966: Lecturer and Deputy Director of the independent Department of Psychology; 1966–: Head of the Department of Psychology

(Continued)

Table 5: (Continued)

Name	Date of birth	Year/place of degree obtained	Dissertation title	Scientific area	Workplace
Lajos Duró	1928	1957 Soviet Union	The education of proletarian nationality in the educational process (based on the teaching of history) in the upper classes of Soviet and Hungarian schools	general psychology	1957–1958: Ministry of Education, Department of Secondary Education – Lecturer; 1958–1961: PTI Department of Educational Theory – research associate; 1960–1970: Associate Professor, Department of Educational Science and Psychology, University of Szeged
György Geréb	1923	1957	Main features of Comenius' didactic views	labour psychology	1949–1963: Szeged Teacher Training College, Department of Educational Science 1963–1982: Organizes and heads the Department of Psychology
Ferenc Hepp	1909	1960	Main issues in the perception of sport movements	pedagogical psychology	1959–1969: Director of the Institute for Scientific Research in Physical Education; 1969–: Professor at the College of Physical Education

Name	Date of birth	Year/place of degree obtained	Dissertation title	Scientific area	Workplace
Edit S. Molnár	1934	1963	Educational psychology of understanding a literary text	pedagogical psychology	1957–: Teacher of psychology and logic at the Buda High School; 1960s: Arany János Primary School – teacher, Second half of the 1960s: Hungarian Radio Opinion Research Department
István Molnár	1928	1965 Soviet Union	Some characteristics of pubertal independence (based on their judgements)	pedagogical psychology	1959–1961: teacher at the teacher training college; 1965–: Research fellow at the Institute of Psychology of the Hungarian Academy of Sciences
László Nagy	1932	1965	Psychological characteristics of the practical application of knowledge in solving physical tasks	pedagogical psychology	1958–: Teacher Training Institute teacher; 1962–1965: ELTE Department of Psychology 1966–: Associate Professor, Országos Pedagógiai Intézet (OPI – National Pedagogical Institute)
Jenő Putnoky	1928	1965	The role of explicit word reactions to mediating processes in the development of generalisation and differentiation in 6–10-year-olds	general psychology	1952–1960: elementary and secondary school teacher, supervisor; 1963–1973: ELTE Department of General Psychology – senior lecturer; 1973–1981: Associate Professor

(Continued)

Table 5: (Continued)

Name	Date of birth	Year/place of degree obtained	Dissertation title	Scientific area	Workplace
Pál Rókus-falvy	1931	1966	Career maturity of students choosing a career. Psychological problems of preparing for career choice	labour psychology	1956–1960: MÁV Aptitude Test Station – psychologist; 1960–1963: Head of the Motor Transport Aptitude Testing Laboratory; 1963–1970: MTA Institute of Psychology – research fellow
Jenő Salamon	1930	1958 Soviet Union (Moscow)	Age specificity of elementary constructive activity of schoolchildren (first, third, fifth grades)	development psychology	1958–1961: staff member of the PTI; 1961– Head of the Department of Psychology, ELTE; 1973–: Head of the Department of Developmental and Educational Psychology at ELTE
Béla Tóth	1913	1966	A psychological study of primary school pupils' interest in literature	pedagogical psychology	1952–1959: teacher at the Budapest Teacher Training Institute; 1967–1978: OPI Department of Pedagogy

The migration of educational psychology researchers from education sciences to psychology occurred not only among candidates, but also among academic doctors (Table 6). In 1962, there were no academic doctors in psychology, but by 1970, the number had risen to five (Almanac, 1973).[22] According to the

22 Academic doctors in psychology in 1970: Lajos Bartha (developmental psychology), László Gábor Horváth (labour psychology), Lajos Kardos (educational psychology), László Kelemen (educational psychology), and Ferenc Lénárd (general psychology, child and educational psychology).

categorisation of the Academic Almanac, three of the five academic doctors were classified in the field of educational psychology, namely Lajos Kardos, László Kelemen, and Ferenc Lénárd. Although the term developmental psychology is noted next to Lajos Bartha's name, his work aligns him with educational psychology research. Notably, Bartha was the only academic doctor of educational psychology who obtained both his academic doctorate and his candidate's degree in the Soviet Union, which influenced his Soviet psychologically orientation. Ferenc Lénárd, who obtained both his candidate title and his academic doctorate in the field of psychology, as well as his academic doctorate and had a keen interest in educational psychology, can also be considered as a member of this group of researchers.

The separation of psychology from education sciences is illustrated by the fact that Lajos Kardos was still a general psychological researcher in the field of educational science in 1962, but by 1970 he had already transitioned to psychology. However, his discipline classification still acknowledges his contribution to educational psychology (Almanac, 1970). However, this migration does not coincide with that of educational psychology researchers, as Kardos was already a psychologist before 1956, and his work reflected influences from Western psychology rather than Soviet. For Kardos, this relevance of Western psychology was also evident in his scientific recruitment practices, as he directed his students towards Western, primarily American psychology research (Hunyady, 1996; Pléh, 2016). The definitive separation of Kardos from education sciences occurred in the early 1970s, when the 1973 Academic Almanac no longer categorised him as a researcher of educational psychology, but of general psychology (Almanac, 1973).

In summary, it can be claimed that by the early 1970s, researchers who had obtained their candidate titles in educational psychology in the late 1950s, and their academic doctorates in psychology in the late 1960s and early 1970s, emerged as prominent figures among academic doctors in psychology. This group included Lajos Bartha, László Kelemen, and Jenő Salamon, as well as Ferenc Lénárd. All of them began their professional careers at the Pedagogical Scientific Institute in the second half of the 1950s, representing Soviet-style psychology within the broader field, and were regarded as the "founding fathers" of Hungarian socialist educational psychology. In contrast, they were counterbalanced by the Western-oriented psychologist Lajos Kardos.

Table 6: Academic doctors in psychology specialised in pedagogy in 1970 (own editing)

Name	Date of birth	Year/place of degree obtained	Dissertation title	Scientific area	Workplace
Lajos Bartha	1927	1959 Soviet Union	Education for professional dedication in the military officer schools	developmental psychology	1959–1961: staff member of the Pedagogical Scientific Institute (PTI); 1960–1962: Associate Professor, Department of Psychology, ELTE; 1962: Director of the Psychology Institute of the Hungarian Academy of Sciences
Lajos Kardos	1899	1955	Pavlov's research and psychology	educational psychology	1963–1971: Head of the Department of Psychology, ELTE
László Kelemen	1919	1957	Concepts and thinking in lower primary school	educational psychology	1948: lecturer and head of the Department of Education at the Teacher Training College of Pécs; 1964–1966: Head of the independent Department of Psychology; 1966–1981: Founder and Head of the Department of Educational Science and later of the Department of Psychology at the University of Debrecen

Name	Date of birth	Year/place of degree obtained	Dissertation title	Scientific area	Workplace
Ferenc Lénárd	1911	1961	Problem-solving thinking	general psychology, child and educational psychology	1954–1962: PTI staff member; 1962–1972: Psychology Institute of the Hungarian Academy of Sciences

Conclusions

Until the end of the Stalinist-era in 1956, the pursuit of psychology was prohibited across the socialist bloc, including Hungary. However, from 1956 onwards, in the post-Stalin era, it became possible to cultivate psychology and educational psychology. In Hungary, at the end of the 1950s, researchers with an education psychology orientation obtained their candidate titles in the field of educational science, but by the late 1960s, they shifted to psychology. This migration also occurred among academic doctors. This transition meant that educational psychology researchers moved away from educational science, carving out a distinct niche within the field of psychology. The result of this process was the establishment of Hungarian socialist educational psychology in the second half of the 1960s.

From the point of view of scientific recruitment, the result by the end of the 1960s was that researchers in educational psychology were no longer integrated into education sciences, but affiliated themselves with the field of psychology. In this way, research in educational psychology contributed to enriching psychology rather than education sciences. This marked the beginning of educational psychology as a permanent part of psychology, as it is today.

These processes did not occur without conflict, which is reflected in the dynamics between educational science and psychology, and within the field of psychology itself. In the 1950s, the young field of socialist education ignored psychology, dismissing it as a bourgeois science. In contrast, from the 1960s, the representatives of Western psychology, newly freed from the shadow of censorship, produced their own critiques of education sciences and socialist educational psychology. They argued that both were inherently socialist in orientation and content, asserting that educational psychology was merely a "ripped-off" of socialist education sciences. The rift between psychologists and educational psychologists continues to this day, though it is no longer driven by ideological conflict, as educational psychology is not the most dynamically developing area within psychology.

In terms of scientific recruitment, this also has important implications: researchers in psychology PhD programmes tend to choose more traditional fields (e.g., social psychology or developmental psychology) or newer approaches (e.g., cognitive psychology), as opposed to educational psychology.

Bibliography

Akadémiai Almanach (1962). *A Magyar Tudományos Akadémia Almanachja.* Akadémiai Kiadó. https://real-j.mtak.hu/3088/1/Almanach_1962.pdf

Akadémiai Almanach (1967). *A Magyar Tudományos Akadémia Almanachja.* Akadémiai Kiadó. https://real-j.mtak.hu/3089/1/Almanach_1967.pdf

Akadémiai Almanach (1970). *A Magyar Tudományos Akadémia Almanachja.* Akadémiai Kiadó. https://real-j.mtak.hu/3090/1/Almanach_1970.pdf

Akadémiai Almanach (1973). *A Magyar Tudományos Akadémia Almanachja.* Akadémiai Kiadó. https://real-j.mtak.hu/3091/1/Almanach_1973.pdf

Akadémiai Értesítő (1952–1972). *A Magyar Tudományos Akadémia Értesítője.* Akadémiai Kiadó. https://real-j.mtak.hu/view/journal/Akad=E9miai_=C9rtes=EDt==0151_=2F_Magyar_Tudom=E1ny.html

Báthory, Z., & Falus, I. (Eds.). (1997). *Pedagógiai Lexikon* (Vol. 1–3). Keraban.

Brezsnyánszky, L. (2015). Kontinuitás és diszkontinuitás a debreceni egyetem pedagógia oktatóinak rekrutációjában 1940–1970. In A. Németh, Zs. H. Biró, & I. Garai (Eds.), *Neveléstudomány és tudományos elit a 20. század második felében* (pp. 225–251). Gondolat Kiadó. https://real.mtak.hu/35462/1/Nevelestudomany_törd_1.pdf

Darvai, T. (2019). A szocialista neveléslélektan megteremtése Magyarországon az 1960-as években. *Iskolakultúra, 29*(8), 47–67. https://doi.org/10.14232/ISKKULT.2019.8.47

Fizel, N. (2014). Sík Sándor szerepe a párhuzamos tanszékek megalakulásában a Ferenc József Tudományegyetemen. In P. Miklós (Ed.), *Sík Sándor eszmekörei* (pp. 63–75). Radnóti Szegedi Öröksége Alapítvány.

Fizel, N. (2018). *A magyar polgári iskolai tanárképzés története (1868–1947).* Gondolat Kiadó.

Fitzpatrick, S. (Ed.). (2000). *Stalinism: New Directions.* Routledge.

Golnhofer, E., & Szabolcs, É. (2013). Lázár György és a magyar pedológia – mítosz és valóság. *Magyar Pedagógia, 113*(3), 133–151. https://www.magyarpedagogia.hu/index.php/magyarpedagogia/article/view/60/60

Hunyady, Gy. (1996). A budapesti tudományegyetem és a pszichológia. *Magyar Pszichológiai Szemle, 52*(1–3), 3–16. https://real-j.mtak.hu/5286/1/MagyarPszichologiaiSzemle_52.pdf

Jones, P. (2006). Introduction: the dilemmas of de-Stalinization. In P. Jones (Ed.), *The Dilemmas of De-Stalinization: Negotiating Cultural and Social Changes in the Khrushchev era* (pp. 1–19). Routledge.

Joravsky, D. (1989). *Russian psychology: A critical history*. Blackwell.

Karády, V. (2015). Egy szocialista értelmiségi „államnemesség"? Kandidátusok és akadémiai doktorok a hazai társadalomtudományokban. In A. Németh, Zs. H. Biró, & I. Garai (Eds.), *Neveléstudomány és tudományos elit a 20. század második felében* (pp. 251–281). Gondolat Kiadó. https://real.mtak.hu/35462/1/Nevelestudomany_törd_1.pdf

Kardos, L. (1952). Hozzászólás egy neveléslélektani tanulmány vitájához. *Pedagógiai Szemle, 2*(1–2), 102–119.

Kardos, L. (1955). Pavlov kutatásai és a lélektan. Doktori értekezés tézisei. *Pedagógiai Szemle, 5*(5–6), 546–549.

Kerékgyártó, I. (1952). A logikus gondolkodás fejlesztése a nyelvtan tanításának keretében. *Pedagógiai Szemle, 2*(1–2), 90–101.

Knausz, I. (1986). A magyar „pedológia" pere. *Pedagógiai Szemle, 36*(11), 1087–1102.

Knausz, I. (1994). *A közoktatás Magyarországon 1945–1956*. Kandidátusi disszertáció. https://mek.oszk.hu/10000/10080/10080.pdf

Kovai, M. (2016). *Lélektan és politika: pszichotudományok a magyarországi államszocializmusban, 1945–1970*. L'Harmattan.

Kotkin, S. (1995) *Magnetic Mountain: Stalinism as a Civilization*. University of California Press.

Lázár, Gy. (1950). A magyar pedológia visszavonulási taktikája. *Társadalmi Szemle, 5*(3–4), 250–276.

Lénárd, E., & Baranyai, E. (1951). A logikai gondolkodás fejlesztése a számtan és nyelvtan tanításának keretében. *Pedagógiai Szemle, 1*(1–2), 46–100.

Lénárd, E., & Baranyai, E. (1952). Válasz újabb hozzászólásokra és a vita tanulságai. *Pedagógiai Szemle, 2*(3), 247–263.

Mihály, O. (1999). Fordulat és pedagógia. In O. Mihály (Ed.), *Az emberi minőség esélyei: pedagógiai tanulmányok* (pp. 234–278). Okker.

Nagy, S. (Ed.). (1976–1979). *Pedagógiai Lexikon* (Vol. 1–4). Akadémiai Kiadó.

N. A. (1952). Egy neveléslélektani vita tanulságai. *Pedagógiai Szemle, 2*(6), 562–572.

N. A. (1957). Sokrétűen és alaposan tanulmányozzuk a gyermeket. *Pedagógiai Szemle, 7*(1) 8–14.

Pénzes, D. (2013). A tudományos fokozatszerzés átalakulása 1948–1953 között Magyarországon. In G. Baska, J. Hegedűs, & A. Nóbik (Eds.), *A neveléstörténet változó arcai* (pp. 69–80). ELTE Eötvös Kiadó. https://www.eltereader.hu/media/2014/02/Hegedus_READER.pdf

Pénzes, D. (2016). A hazai pedagógia szaksajtó-kutatás történetéhez: A Pedagógiai Szemle genezise. *Neveléstudomány | Oktatás – Kutatás – Innováció, 4*(3), 36–48. https://doi.org/10.21549/NTNY.15.2016.3.3

Péter, A. (Ed.). (1954). *Az SzKP, a Szovjet Kormány és a Komszomol határozatai a szovjet iskoláról.* Tankönyvkiadó.

Pléh, Cs. (1998). A pszichológia szimbolikája egy slampos totalitárius rendszerben. A magyar pszichológia a hatvanas években. In Cs. Pléh (Ed.), *Hagyomány és újítás a pszichológiában* (pp. 91–111). Balassi Kiadó.

Pléh, Cs. (2016). Intézmények, eszmék és sorsok a magyar pszichológia fél évszázadában 1960–2010. *Magyar Pszichológiai Szemle, 71*(4–5), 691–723. https://doi.org/10.1556/0016.2016.71.4.5

Pukánszky, B. (2021). Pedagógia és lélektan a szegedi egyetemen, 1872–1945. In Á. Szokolszky (Ed.), *A pszichológia fejlődése a vidéki Magyarországon a kezdetektől a rendszerváltás utáni évekig* (pp. 85–99). JATE Press. https://acta.bibl.u-szeged.hu/72216/1/pszichologia_fejlodese_2021.pdf

Rainer M., J. (2011). *Bevezetés a kádárizmusba.* L'Harmattan.

Sáska, G. (2005). A társadalmi egyenlőség antikapitalista és demokrácia-ellenes képzete a XX. századi pedagógiai ideológiákban. *Magyar Pedagógia, 105*(1), 83–99. https://www.magyarpedagogia.hu/index.php/magyarpedagogia/article/view/324/322

Sáska, G. (2008). A reformpedagógia alakváltozása az 1945-ös „kis" és az 1947 utáni „nagy" rendszerváltást követő időszakban. *Iskolakultúra, 28*(1–2), 3–23. https://www.iskolakultura.hu/index.php/iskolakultura/article/view/20709/20499

Sáska, G. (2009). A szocialista neveléstudomány kialakulása és függősorba süllyedése – a didaktika példáján. In A. Németh, & Zs. H. Biró (Eds.), *A magyar neveléstudomány a XX. század második felében* (pp. 98–130). Gondolat Kiadó.

Sáska, G. (2011). *Új társadalomhoz új embert és új pedagógiát!.* Gondolat Kiadó. http://mek.niif.hu/14000/14077/14077.pdf

Sáska, G. (2015a). A neveléstudományi elit viszonya a politikai marxizmushoz az ötvenes években. In A. Németh, Zs. H. Biró, & I. Garai (Eds.), *Neveléstudomány és tudományos elit a 20. század második felében* (pp. 177–212). Gondolat Kiadó. https://real.mtak.hu/35462/1/Nevelestudomany_törd_1.pdf

Sáska, G. (2015b). A pedagógiai normák változása az 1920-as 30-as évek Szovjet-Oroszországában. *Pedagógiatörténeti Szemle, 1*(1), 31–52. https://epa.oszk.hu/04000/04018/00002/pdf/EPA04018_pedagogiatorteneti_szemle_2015_01_31-52.pdf

Sáska, G. (2016). A szocialista neveléstudomány rekrutációja 1956–1962 között. In P. Tóth, & I. Holik (Eds.), *Új kutatások a neveléstudományokban 2015. Pedagógusok, tanulók, iskolák – az értékformálás, az értékközvetítés és az értékteremtés világa* (pp. 255–262). ELTE Eötvös Kiadó. https://www.eltereader.hu/media/2016/12/UKN_2016_WEB.pdf

Sáska G. (2017). Embernek lenni sötét időkben. A neveléstudomány és marxizmus-leninizmus a sztálini korban. In A. Németh, & B. Pukánszky (Eds.), *Gyermekek, tanárok, iskolák – egykoron és ma. Tanulmányok a 90 éves Mészáros István tiszteletére* (pp. 165–176). ELTE Eötvös Kiadó. https://www.eltereader.hu/media/2017/05/Nemeth_Meszaros_tiszt_kot_WEB.pdf

Attila Czabaji Horváth,[1] Zsófia Albrecht,[2] Andrea Daru,[2]
Dorina Szente,[3] Györgyi Vincze[4]

Contributions to the question of scientific qualifications in the field of education in Hungary between 1970 and 1990

Abstract: In our paper, we focus on the emergence of a later generation of scientists, referred to as the scientific offspring, examining their training, entry into the scientific field, chosen topics, and the knowledge constructs that they created. The study covers the two decades from 1970 to the regime change. During his period, a 'Soviet-style' system of academic qualifications, introduced in 1950, was in operation, the characteristics of which have been discussed in several studies (see Czabaji et al., 2023; Fortescue, 1986; Glatz, 2002; Kozári, 2015; Znepolski, 2020). By examining the outputs of this new generation of scientists under the Soviet-style system, we aim to analyse the defining condition for entry into the academic field, the candidate's dissertation, with a particular focus on the accompanying thesis booklets. In this paper, we address three selected research questions, one of which is discussed in greater detail as our corpus analysis is still ongoing.

Keywords: scientific recruitment, academic qualification, candidates.

Introduction

Our analysis is primarily based on Stichweh's concept of discipline, which considers the individuals involved in the creation of scientific products as integral parts of science itself. The discipline, as defined by Stichweh, consists of four

1 Institute of Education, ELTE Eötvös Loránd University, Budapest, Hungary, horvath.h.attila@ppk.elte.hu

2 Doctoral School of Education, ELTE Eötvös Loránd University, Budapest, Hungary, albrecht.zsofia@ppk.elte.hu; daru.andrea@music.unideb.hu

3 Department of Pedagogy and Psychology, Hungarian Dance University, Budapest, Hungary, szente.dorina@mte.eu

4 Bárczi Gusztáv Faculty of Special Needs Education, ELTE Eötvös Loránd University, Budapest, Hungary, vincze.gyorgyi@barczi.elte.hu

components: a) the institutional infrastructure of research, b) the network of scientific communication, c) the cognitive products (i.e., scientific creations) of the discipline, and d) the education and professional socialisation of the scientific offspring (Stichweh, 1992).

We utilize Bourdieu's field theory as the theoretical framework to closely examine the scientific offspring. According to Bourdieu (2005, p. 63.), scientists, through specific socialisation processes, 'constantly adapt themselves to the expectations imposed by the field,' to which they are active contributors. Understanding and adhering to the rules of the field is crucial for establishing oneself within the scientific community. Bourdieu also notes that a key function of any disciplinary field is the continuous transmission of scientific knowledge to the next generation, involving the training and professional socialisation of new specialists (Bourdieu, 2005, p. 173). The field also serves as a battleground where criteria for evaluation and formal classification are both contested and regulated. It should be noted, however, that the applicability of this theory to the regulation of academic life under socialism is limited (Szabó, 2016, pp. 204–205).

Research questions

Based on the theoretical background introduced above, we addressed the following research questions:

1. What themes and scientific views do new entrants to the field of education choose during the two decades examined?
2. To what extent are the authors who obtained their degrees during this period represented in the two leading journals of Hungarian educational science, *Magyar Pedagógia* (Hungarian Pedagogy) and *Iskolakultúra* (School Culture)?
3. How is the Scientific-Technological Revolution (STR), a significant current during the period examined, represented in the discourse on academic qualifications?

Methods

Doctoral dissertations are a critical source of information for analysing the professional performance of junior researchers. However, for our study, we have chosen to use thesis booklets instead, due to both content-related and practical considerations. Content-wise, thesis booklets substantially condense the dissertations, while practically speaking, the process of digitising texts is more feasible with booklets, typically eleven pages long as opposed to dissertations, which can range from 150–160 pages.

We included seventy thesis booklets from successful doctoral dissertations of the period in our study corpus. These materials were processed using data mining and content analysis, for which we constructed a dictionary using both inductive and deductive approaches. In the deductive approach, we began with the categorisation systems of Tenorth (2001) and Németh and Biró (2009). We also utilised a well-known series of the period, the *Társadalomtudományi Könyvtár* [Social Sciences Library], as well as Babbie's (2001) methodological division of the field to develop categories for content and methodological analysis. In the inductive approach, we developed concepts by thoroughly reading through the contents of the thesis booklets. The analysis and interpretation of the data were performed using the text analysis software ATLAS.ti.

Results

Themes and scientific views of new entrants (scientific offspring)

From 1970 to 1990, a total of 172 successful doctoral theses were submitted in the field of education. Grouping these theses by topic reveals that more than a quarter of these (46) focused on the study of specific types of schools; of these, the majority (25) examined primary schools.

Moral education was the focus of two papers, while others addressed aesthetic and family life education. Special attention was given to themes including student activity, social democracy, and social engagement. The authors emphasised the importance of preparing students for social contribution starting in primary school, with some even advocating for the establishment of a pedagogical foundation for socialist responsibility beginning in lower primary education. Notable issues included the education of children in housing estates and the education for health-conscious behavior.

The analysis, facilitated by our dictionary, revealed that dissertations on the history of education represent the largest category, with a total of 20 dissertations. These cover a broad spectrum of topics, ranging from the early 20th-century work of the reform educator László Nagy (1857–1931) to the Szalkai Codex (1489–90), and include studies on 18th-century colleges and the pedagogical and agricultural innovations introduced by Baron Sámuel Tessedik (1742–1820).

In the period leading up to the regime change and democratic transformation, topics such as the trade union policy of the Magyar Dolgozók Pártja [Hungarian Working People's Party], the public education policies of Gyula Kornis (1885–1958), and the history of social science education in the United States were also explored.

Nearly 10% of the dissertations focus on the teaching of foreign languages, with some overlap with those on general education. Many of these writings are related to Russian in particular, which was a compulsory language during this period. Notably, two significant works stand out in addition to studies on minority languages: one specifically addressed the teaching of English using a communicative language pedagogy approach, while another examined the historical methods of teaching foreign languages, with a focus on Anglo-Saxon examples.

We also examined the scientific viewpoints presented in the theses. During this period, the prevailing and expected worldview within the socialist camp was Marxism-Leninism, accompanied by dialectical materialism in the scientific realm. As expected, the analysis of the theses demonstrates the prevalence of this approach. However, other paradigms were also mentioned and deliberated upon. These included a notable coexistence of:

- dialectical materialism (183 mentions, ratio: 0.19),
- critical sociology (126 mentions, ratio: 0.16),
- structuralism (112 mentions, ratio: 0.14),
- cognitivism (81 mentions, ratio: 0.14),
- systems theory (81 mentions, ratio: 0.14).

Table 1: The distribution of the dictionary's categories (own editing)

	1968–1969		1970–1974		1975–1979		1980–1984		1985–1989		1990–1994		1995–1999		2000–2004		2005–2009		2010–2014		2015–2018		Totals	
	Absolute	Row-relative	Absolute	Row-relative	Absolute	Row-relative	Absolute	Row-relative	Absolute	Row-relative	Absolute	Row-relative	Absolute	Row-relative	Absolute	Row-relative	Absolute	Row-relative	Absolute	Row-relative	Absolute	Row-relative	Absolute	Row-relative
figuration theory	9	4,46%	25	12,38%	29	14,36%	31	15,35%	16	7,92%	15	7,43%	18	8,91%	22	10,89%	17	8,42%	11	5,45%	9	4,46%	202	100,00%
dialectical materialism	45	8,75%	134	26,07%	134	26,07%	91	17,70%	49	9,53%	11	2,14%	24	4,67%	12	2,34%	6	1,17%	4	0,78%	4	0,78%	514	100,00%
phenomenology	2	4,08%	2	4,08%	2	4,08%	10	20,41%	3	6,12%	2	4,08%	8	16,33%	9	18,37%	2	4,08%	4	8,16%	5	10,20%	49	100,00%
functionalism	0	0,00%	2	3,18%	4	6,35%	13	20,63%	4	6,35%	5	7,94%	5	7,94%	9	14,29%	8	12,70%	5	7,94%	8	12,70%	63	100,00%
cognitivism	22	5,40%	58	14,25%	47	11,55%	41	10,07%	39	9,58%	23	5,65%	50	12,29%	52	12,78%	29	7,12%	25	6,14%	21	5,16%	407	100,00%
critical theory	0	0,00%	3	6,82%	0	0,00%	1	2,27%	6	13,64%	7	15,91%	1	2,27%	13	29,55%	4	9,09%	1	2,27%	8	18,18%	44	100,00%
critical sociology	36	5,56%	117	18,08%	103	15,92%	83	12,83%	65	10,05%	36	5,56%	51	7,88%	58	8,96%	38	5,87%	37	5,72%	23	3,55%	647	100,00%
field theory	2	5,00%	3	7,50%	12	30,00%	8	20,00%	4	10,00%	0	0,00%	3	7,50%	2	5,00%	0	0,00%	2	5,00%	4	10,00%	40	100,00%
positivism	5	3,50%	19	13,29%	18	12,59%	21	14,69%	14	9,79%	9	6,29%	11	7,69%	16	11,19%	4	2,80%	12	8,39%	14	9,79%	143	100,00%
pragmatism	18	6,34%	38	13,38%	28	9,86%	37	13,03%	30	10,56%	24	8,45%	39	13,73%	31	10,91%	15	5,28%	12	4,22%	12	4,22%	284	100,00%
systems theory	0	0,00%	8	4,97%	46	28,57%	42	26,09%	13	8,08%	3	1,86%	15	9,32%	4	2,48%	5	3,11%	9	5,59%	16	9,94%	161	100,00%
structuralism	11	2,62%	48	11,46%	62	14,80%	74	17,66%	41	9,79%	33	7,88%	35	8,35%	47	11,22%	24	5,73%	18	4,30%	26	6,20%	419	100,00%
humanities	1	2,08%	2	4,17%	1	2,08%	8	16,67%	4	8,33%	4	8,33%	9	18,75%	8	16,67%	4	8,33%	4	8,33%	3	6,25%	48	100,00%
symbolic interactionism	1	5,26%	1	5,26%	3	15,79%	0	0,00%	3	15,79%	1	5,26%	2	10,53%	2	10,53%	0	0,00%	3	15,79%	3	15,79%	19	100,00%
social systems	0	0,00%	0	0,00%	1	12,50%	0	0,00%	0	0,00%	1	12,50%	1	12,50%	2	25,00%	1	12,50%	0	0,00%	2	25,00%	8	100,00%
Totals	152	4,99%	460	15,09%	490	16,08%	460	15,09%	291	9,55%	174	5,71%	272	8,92%	287	9,42%	157	5,15%	147	4,82%	158	5,18%	3048	100,00%

When examining the presence of different scientific trends in the journal *Magyar Pedagógia* [Hungarian Pedagogy] over time, we observed a notable decline specifically in dialectical materialism, whereas the other trends present a more balanced picture. Between 1970 and 1989, the representation of dialectical materialism in the studies decreased by over 16%. There was also a decline in cognitivism, critical sociology, and structuralism; though critical sociology saw the largest decrease among those mentioned above, this was only about half of the decline observed for dialectical materialism. Conversely, systems theory demonstrated resilience, showing a slight rise at the lower end (3%) and a more significant increase in the intermediate period (over 20%).

The pedagogical discourse of the time was heavily influenced and predetermined by ideology, reflecting the power dynamics and the necessity or desire to align with it. As disillusionment with ideology grew and the political landscape approached a turning point, this shift became evident in the scientific literature as well.

Table 2: The presence of scientific trends in the studies of Magyar Pedagógia between 1970 and 1989 (own editing)

	1970–1974		**1975–1979**		**1980–1984**		**1985–1989**	
	Absolute	**Row-relative**	**Absolute**	**Row-relative**	**Absolute**	**Row-relative**	**Absolute**	**Row-relative**
dialectical materialism	134	26,07%	134	26,07%	91	17,70%	49	9,53%
cognitivism	58	14,25%	47	11,55%	41	10,07%	39	9,58%
critical sociology	117	18,08%	103	15,92%	83	12,83%	65	10,05%
systems theory	8	4,97%	46	28,57%	42	26,09%	13	8,08%
structuralism	48	11,46%	62	14,80%	74	17,66%	41	9,79%
Totals	460	15,09%	490	16,08%	460	15,09%	291	9,55%

Activity of new entrants in the field of education

We were also interested in determining the extent to which individuals who obtained their doctoral degrees during the study period became active practitioners in the field of education. To explore this, we examined their publication records in two journals, *Magyar Pedagógia* and *Iskolakultúra* [School Culture], up to the present day. While this approach does not provide a complete answer, it offers insights into their publication activities in prominent Hungarian educational science journals.

Out of the 172 candidates, 67 had no publications in the analysed journals (six of whom were foreigners), while 26 had only one publication. This suggests that around half of those who earned a doctoral degree in education during the period did not demonstrate significant activity in their field of study based on these criteria.

This phenomenon can largely be attributed to the specific nature of the rating system, in which political-ideological conformity was a significant factor alongside professional requirements. While individual motivations and ambitions may also have played a role, we posit that these factors had less of an explanatory effect compared to ideological alignment.

Table 3: Number of publications in the Magyar Pedagógia and Iskolakultúra journals from 1970 to the present day by persons who received a doctorate in education between 1970 and 1990 (own editing)

Number of publications	Number of authors	%	Note
0	67	39,8	Six foreigners
1	26	15	
2–5	34	19,7	
6–10	16	9	
11–19	16	9	
20–	13	7,5	Three with over 40 publications

The imprints of the Scientific and Technological Revolution in thesis booklets

The Scientific-Technological Revolution (STR) has been a key factor in the rapid development of 20th century economy and society. As Kalmár states, '[…] *in the pioneering countries, its effects were felt as early as the 1950s and 1960s, not only in the inspiring military industry and at macroeconomic levels, but in everyday life and in the whole way of life of the 20th century man*' (Kalmár, 2014, p. 73). The concept of STR appeared in political and in the more restricted professional discourses in the Eastern bloc, including Hungary, during these decades. However, it became widely recognised '*when the advanced industrial societies reached the second round in the early 1970s*' (Kalmár, 2014, p. 73). The two opposing world systems created '*different dimensions of interpretation of the STR phenomenon, exploring its possible economic and social implications. The common cross-cutting theme of all approaches may be a greater regard for the results of science, a belief in scientific, a strengthening of a kind of scientism*' (Somogyvári & Polyák, 2022, p. 112).

During the period under study, the concept and impact of the STR permeated all aspects of life, including work, education, and daily routines. This rapid advancement in science and technology posed challenges and created issues across various domains.

In an earlier pilot study where we examined 40 thesis booklets (see Czabaji et al., 2022), 15 of them included manifestations of the STR intertwined with reflections on the societal processes of the time. There was significant societal interest in ensuring that individuals could keep pace with technological developments, which emphasised the importance of understanding and applying the latest technical achievements, integrating them into education, teaching technology itself, and disseminating technical knowledge.

As highlighted by Somogyvári and Polyák (2022), '*the solution was to be found in polytechnic education* [...] *on the Soviet model*' (Somogyvári & Polyák, 2022, p. 126). Technical education (see Somogyvári & Polyák, 2023) was considered a central component of general education; as such, technical themes are prominently featured across a wide spectrum of dissertations. These range from subject-specific pedagogy (e.g., technology, mathematics, or computing) to technical vocational training (e.g., polytechnics and higher technical education), including the use of tools such as school TV, video, and other audiovisual technologies.

Analysis of these texts underscores that advancing general education is inseparable from scientific and technical progress. Furthermore, the dissertations underscore the challenge posed by the rapid pace of technological development, which can swiftly transform professions and job roles, often outpacing educational curricula and training programs.

Conclusion

Sovietisation impacted scientific qualifications by taking powers previously held by universities and transferring them to a centralised body known as the Scientific Qualifications Board which imposed both professional and ideological requirements on candidates. In the social sciences, particularly education, adherence to a Marxist-Leninist approach was rigorously enforced, in contrast to the natural sciences. Candidates entering the scientific field were cautious of ideological implications, mindful of the potential risk to their years of work and their future careers, as the Scientific Qualifications Board held ideological veto power until the regime change. Although the ideological influence gradually waned, the Soviet model of scientific certification persisted until 1993.

In our examination of doctoral theses from the period, we explored the context in which the Scientific-Technological Revolution (STR) emerged. Candidates echoed political leadership's view that enhancing general education standards is inseparable from scientific and technical progress, emphasising the increasingly technical nature of educational content. The challenges posed by the STR underscored the global importance of education, both in the West and the East. In Hungary, those preparing for careers in education concurred with administrative views that polytechnic education was a suitable response, yet they reported persistent shortcomings.

Professions and job roles have evolved significantly due to scientific and technological advancements, yet the Hungarian education system has struggled to keep pace. This trend has accelerated beyond the period examined in this study and continues to be relevant today. It is important to note that our findings are based on a subset of data from our corpus; a comprehensive review of the entire corpus could provide a more nuanced perspective.

Bibliography

Bourdieu, P. (2005). *A tudomány tudománya és a reflexivitás*. Gondolat Kiadó.

Czabaji Horváth, A., Albrecht, Z., Daru, A., & Szente, D. (2022). Az utánpótlásképzés a neveléstudományban (1970–1993) mint társadalmi jelenség megközelítési lehetőségei. *Múltunk*, *67*(3), 132–168. https://doi.org/10.56944/multunk.2022.3.5

Czabaji Horváth, A., Albrecht, Z., Daru, A., & Szente, D. (2023). Professionalism vs. Ideologization in the Hungarian Candidate Dissertations in Educational Science in the 1970s. *Historia Scholastica*, *9*(1), 207–222. https://doi.org/10.15240/tul/006/2023-1-010

Fortescue, S. (1986). *The Communist Party and Soviet Science*. Springer. https://doi.org/10.1007/978-1-349-08059-5

Glatz, F. (2002). Akadémia és tudománypolitika a volt szocialista országokban 1922–1999. *Magyar Tudomány*, *68*(4), 494–506. https://real.mtak.hu/35354/1/2002_Glatz_Akademia_es_tudomanypolitika_a_volt_szocialista_orszagokban_19221999_u.pdf

Horn, K.-P., & Tenorth, H.-E. (2001). Erziehungswissenschaft in Deutschland in der ersten Hälfte des 20. Jahrhunderts. In K.-P. Horn, A. Németh, B. Pukánszky, & H.-E. Tenorth (Eds.), *Erziehungswissenschaft in Mitteleuropa:*

Aufklärerische Traditionen – deutscher Einfluss – nationale Eigenständigkeit (pp. 176–191). Osiris Kiadó.

Kalmár, M. (2014). *Történelmi galaxisok vonzásában: Magyarország és a szovjetrendszer* (1945–1990). Osiris Kiadó.

Kozári, M. (2015). A tudományos minősítés rendszere Magyarországon az 1940-es évek végétől 1960-ig, az új minősítési rendszer stabilizálódásáig. *Múltunk, 60*(2), 148–194. https://real.mtak.hu/139880/1/kozarim_15_2.pdf

Németh, A., & Biró, Zs. H. (2009). (Eds.). *A magyar neveléstudomány a 20. század második felében*. Gondolat Kiadó.

Németh, A. (2018). *The past and present of the Hungarian educational science – development of a discipline, scientific communication (1970–2017). Research plan*. [Manuscript].

Somogyvári, L., & Polyák, Zs. (2022). A „tudományos-technikai forradalom" diskurzusai a magyar neveléstudományban. *Múltunk, 67*(3), 111–31. https://doi.org/10.56944/multunk.2022.3.4

Somogyvári, L., & Polyák, Zs. (2023). A számítógép és a tudományos-technikai forradalom a pedagógiai diskurzusokban (1968–1977): szerzői és intézményi hátterek. In Zs. Molnár-Kovács, H. Andl, & J. Steklács (Eds.), *21. századi képességek, írásbeliség, esélyegyenlőség* (pp. 48–57). Magyar Tudományos Akadémia Pedagógiai Tudományos Bizottság. https://konferencia.pte.hu/sites/konferencia.pte.hu/files/UKN_2022.pdf

Stichweh, R. (1992). The Sociology of Scientific Disciplines: On the Genesis and Stability of the Disciplinary Structure of Modern Science. *Science in Context*, *5*(1), 3–15. https://doi.org/10.1017/S0269889700001071

Szabó, Z. A. (2016). A jogalkotói szándék egy lehetséges feltérképezési útja a tudományos minősítés szabályozási rendszerében – az előterjesztői indokolások köre (1949–1989). In A. Németh, I. Garai, & Z. A. Szabó (Eds.): *Neveléstudomány és pedagógiai kommunikáció a szocializmus időszakában* (pp. 203–233). Gondolat Kiadó. https://real.mtak.hu/39151/1/PTE_Nemeth_javitott.pdf

Znepolski, I. (2020). *Communist, Science, and the University*. Routledge. https://doi.org/10.4324/9781003019879

Erzsébet Golnhofer[1]

A 'moment of autonomy' for higher education pedagogy. The Higher Education Pedagogical Academy: 1970–1972

Abstract: This study examines the upward process of institutionalisation and independence in higher education pedagogy during the late 1960s and early 1970s. Drawing from social history and sociology of science research, it utilizes Rudolf Stichweh's concept of scientific disciplines and analyses the significance of a series of lectures conducted by the Higher Education Pedagogical Research Centre (FPK) established in 1967, as well as the Higher Education Pedagogical Academy (FPA) organised by it. The study assesses how these initiatives' role in defining the institutional framework, personnel background, and expertise of higher education pedagogy. The research concludes that an increasingly open social and scientific-political environment, along with the expanding institutional framework and the involvement of the knowledge elite, played a significant role in the development of higher education pedagogy as an independent discipline.

Keywords: higher education pedagogy, institutionalisation, independence, scientific discipline

Introductory thoughts

From the 1960s onwards, higher education pedagogy emerged as an established and recognised discipline of the educational sciences, evolving within an increasingly professional context. The last two decades have witnessed the institutionalisation and enrichment of content in higher education pedagogy. Both nationally and internationally, there has been a stabilisation and expansion, albeit to varying degrees, of the pool of academics, researchers, developers, and experts working on higher education issues. Institutions dedicated to research and development in higher education have been established which have generated scientific products such as theoretical models and empirical research results exploring various

1 Institute of Education, ELTE Eötvös Loránd University, Budapest, Hungary, erzsebetgolnhofer@gmail.com

phenomena in the field. Additionally, communication networks in higher education pedagogy have been established (e.g., journals, research reports, series, and conferences), as well as various forms of academic training and professional socialisation. Historical research continues to play a crucial role in the development of this discipline. In addition to the comprehensive historical research on higher education pedagogy, several historical studies on the sub-topic of higher education pedagogy have contributed to the knowledge on the development of the discipline, highlighting its past, present, and perspectives. These studies range from traditional works in the spirit of the historiography of ideas to social history, multidisciplinary cultural studies, and studies within the postmodern paradigm (on the changing functions of pedagogical history, see Németh, 2010; 2015). The present paper extends the scope of this partial research by specifically examining the history and lectures of the series of lectures organised by the Research Centre for Higher Education Pedagogy (FPK) under the name Higher Education Pedagogical Academy (FPA) between 1970 and 1972.

Based on the previous considerations, the aim of this research was to explore the role of the FPA in the process of the institutionalisation and enrichment of higher education pedagogy as a specialised field of knowledge. From among the various interpretations of science, my work is primarily based on Rudolf Stichweh's widely-accepted concept of scientific discipline (Stichweh, 1994, 1997; see interpretations of discipline: Németh & Biró, 2016.) According to Stichweh, an independent scientific discipline consists of four closely interconnected components, which I analyse in a narrower context aligning with the subject and sources of my research. I analyse the FPA as an institutional foundation of higher education pedagogy, examining the characteristics of the group of professionals involved in the creation of new knowledge content, as well as the elements of the scientific communication network, including the lectures and publications derived from them. As a detailed analysis and interpretation of the cognitive products of the lecture series would exceed the scope of this study, this topic will only be briefly addressed. Although the issue of scientific succession is important for understanding higher education pedagogy as a discipline, it did not directly appear in the content of the lecture series, and thus its absence is merely noted in the study.

Building on the aforementioned aims, the research framework – considering both the institutional and cognitive elements of the discipline – are linked to three main concepts: the FPA as an institutional framework, the personal background of the lectures, and the topics of the lecture series. This specialised approach focuses on the professionalisation and secondary professionalisation processes within higher education pedagogy in the late 1960s and early 1970s.

The research questions are as follows:

1. What role did the active press organ related to higher education, the *Felsőoktatási Szemle* [Higher Education Review], play in the development of higher education pedagogy?
2. What framework did the existing institutional base of the discipline (the FPK) provide for the cultivation and dissemination of higher education pedagogy?
3. How did the FPA as an institutional framework, as well as the personnel background of the lectures, influence the autonomy of higher education pedagogy?

The research methods applied in this study, grounded in social history and sociology of science, include several approaches: 1. Exploring the literary background related to institutional frameworks and personal backgrounds. 2. Qualitative content analysis of the Higher Education Review and the FPA lecture series. 3. A prosopographical analysis of the FPA lecturers. 4. Narrative methods utilising excerpts from a 1988 interview with Endre Zibolen, the head of the FPK. Primary written sources examined for this study include issues of the Higher Education Review between 1970 and 1972 and volumes of the FPA. Secondary sources consist of academic almanacs, pedagogical lexicons, bibliographies, and relevant scholarly works.

Several factors influenced my choice of topic: Exploring the autonomy of higher education pedagogy in the late 1960s and early 1970s can provide new and relevant knowledge by uncovering the institutional and personal characteristics of the FPA. The feasibility of this research was supported by the availability of the relevant scholarly sources necessary for the investigation. Personal interest and subjective motivation also played significant roles in my decision, as I was involved in organising the FPA as a scientific assistant at the FPK, under the demanding yet supportive guidance of Endre Zibolen and László Jáki. This provided firsthand knowledge of the dedication of the FPK staff and FPA lecturers to the issues of higher education pedagogy and insight into the popularity and publicity-generating impact of the lecture series.

External and internal needs in the development of higher education pedagogy: First steps

From the 1960s onwards, both in Europe and the United States, there was a growing chorus of criticism regarding the effectiveness of higher education, accompanied by calls for reforms from professional, educational policy, and governmental circles. Alongside the rapid socio-economic and scientific-technological developments unfolding after World War II, the expansion of education and the demand for educational reforms affected higher education as well. Tertiary education was increasingly viewed as an engine for economic growth, and there was a strong demand to align mass higher education with the changing social, economic, cultural, and scientific environment, and to implement reforms that were both theoretically and practically grounded. These higher education reforms unfolded at varying paces, exhibiting unique dynamics and tensions across different countries (Geiger, 1980; Halász, 1988; Jensen & Freeman, Jr., 2019; Kozma, 2006; Ladányi, 1999; Polónyi, 2009; Schrecker, 2021). Throughout these processes, it became evident that general pedagogical knowledge alone was insufficient for establishing reforms. There was a need for interdisciplinary scientific analysis related to higher education, encompassing relevant educational, psychological, sociological, and economic research, along with the application of these findings to both theoretical and practical aspects of the field. During this process, the term 'higher education pedagogy' gained recognition in the 1960s, signalling the institutionalisation of a new field of study.

In Hungary, in the late 1960s and the early 1970s, there was a consensus among political, governmental, and professional circles that, in light of economic and social demands as well as the accelerating scientific-technological revolution, education policy needed to be reconceptualised. Acknowledging the validity of the socialist model while at the same time renewing it, effective reform strategies needed to be developed based on domestic and international efforts (Halász, 1988; Kelemen, 2017; Polónyi, 2009;). In line with these expectations, support for the development of higher education, including the unfolding of higher education pedagogy, emerged through the establishment of institutional and personnel backgrounds, along with the provision of regular attention and publicity for higher education issues. The journal of the National Higher Education Council, the Higher Education Review, and the Higher Education Pedagogical Research Centre (FPK) played remarkable roles in this process.

In addition to laying the foundations of 'socialism', the 7th Congress of the Hungarian Socialist Workers' Party (MSZMP) convened in 1959 also included efforts aimed at addressing the problems of higher education. Aligning with the party's education policy, the editorial board of the Higher Education Review outlined a directive in its inaugural 1960 issue, inviting university and college leaders to identify the primary tasks related to higher education as set forth by the Congress resolutions (Editorial Board, 1960). This directive – resembling party propaganda – to popularize the party goals was realised in the coming years not only in the articles of leaders but also in publications written by educators. While the writings initially reflected the goals and ideological perspectives outlined by politics and the party, over time the emphasis on political and ideological control and subordination decreased, creating room for a more professional interest in pedagogy and a broader pedagogical approach to current issues in higher education. Professionals with a heightened interest in higher education pedagogy held varying views regarding the activity of educators in the field. Some claimed a lack of initiatives in this area (e.g., Trencsényi-Waldapfel, 1960), while others noted that recent issues of the Higher Education Review and leading pedagogical journals demonstrated effective engagement with pedagogical issues in higher education, with spontaneous engagement among a wide range of university and college employees in addressing key issues (e.g., Elekes & Zibolen, 1964).

During this period, the development of higher education pedagogy as an independent field of science was not yet clear, with limited societal acceptance, support, and legitimisation for the field. By analysing the list of authors and topics covered in the Higher Education Review, one could discern what the authors, essentially interpreted higher education pedagogy as a distinct field of knowledge. The articles primarily dealt with the following main topics: the goals of higher education (in response to external and internal needs), issues related to the system and institutional organisation of higher education, the personal factors influencing higher education, and the characteristics of university and college teaching. The predominantly classicist interpretation of the discipline played an important role, with little space given to methodological aspects in research, particularly those of a positivist nature. The logic and topics of the studies prioritised practical aims, focusing mainly on supporting practical activities, presenting educators' teaching experiences, the methodological practices of educators in domestic and primarily socialist countries, and their content, methodological endeavours, and research results. The articles indicated a re-evaluation of education, and thus higher education pedagogy, alongside the traditionally specialised sciences.[2]

Some authors emphasised the need for systematic, organised scientific research, highlighting the importance of developing higher education pedagogy (e.g., Bor, 1965; Gerhard, 1963; Lipák, 1964; Némedi, 1960). There was also a strengthening of the perspective that reinforced the prestige of the field: educators in higher education mentioned pedagogical preparedness and the acquisition of applicable pedagogical knowledge as essential conditions for effective work in higher education settings (Elekes & Zibolen, 1964; Faludi & Kóczy, 1964; Hahn, 1970).

---

2 See the transformation of higher education functions (e.g. Kozma, 2006).

Continuing institutionalisation and independence

The development of organised institutional research in higher education in Hungary began as early as the mid-1960s, exerting significant influence on the unfolding of higher education pedagogy. In 1963, the Ministry of Culture and Education (MM) spearheaded the establishment of the Higher Education Pedagogical Research Group (FPKCS) at Eötvös Loránd University, which was tasked with organising higher education pedagogical research. According to the directive of the MM, its members endeavoured to link the study of pedagogical issues in higher education to educational reform and to prepare long-term plans. Their responsibilities included monitoring domestic research in this field, coordinating related plans, and involving the broader professional community through position statements and informative briefs on these plans. These tasks were carried out by the group's internal staff members, who were assigned specific territorial and sectoral assignments by the MM (Elekes & Zibolen, 1964; Ladányi, 2000a; Némedi, 1960; Pečenková, 1967; Zibolen, 1964).

Based on the articles in the Higher Education Review, it appears that the interpretation of higher education pedagogy was still quite fluid, with an ongoing exploration of its boundaries and connections. Alongside external (mainly political) regulation, efforts towards internal regulation and the development of relatively autonomous operations can also be observed (for more on regulation, see, e.g., Baska, 2015; Németh & Biró, 2016). As the discipline matured, there arose a demand for the establishment of a scientifically grounded system of higher education pedagogy that would meet the requirements of pedagogy, psychology, logic, and medicine, as well as socialist societal and economic demands (Lipák, 1964). It might not be an exaggeration to claim that this period marked a shift towards a more open interpretation of interdisciplinary science. In connection with institutionalisation, there was also a noticeable trend aimed at weakening the role of the state and central control, asserting that higher education itself was the sole authority in developing higher education pedagogy. The FPKCS, as a specialised pedagogical research group, was viewed as a body to encourage, support, and coordinate this process rather than dictate it (Faludi & Kóczy, 1964; Sarkadi, 1988, pp. 220–221). Reflecting on the effectiveness of the group, Endre Zibolen, the only main staff member, recalled more than two decades later that the professional output of the group was limited due to the small size of the staff (Sarkadi, 1988, p. 219).

The establishment of the Higher Education Pedagogical Research Centre (FPK) in 1967 marked a decisive moment in the development of the discipline. The FPK, drawing on significant human capital and international experience, provided a platform for broader range of research, service, and informational activities, including hosting conferences, organising scientific meetings, and encouraging publication efforts (See Ladányi, 2000b; Felsőoktatási Pedagógiai Kutatóközpont, 1976). Endre Zibolen, who played a prominent role in operating and directing the FPK, stated in 1967 that '*in the past decade, higher education pedagogy has evolved into one of the fastest-growing branches of pedagogy*' (Zibolen, 1967, p. 537). However, in an interview conducted in 1988, he offered a more nuanced view. He emphasised two significant factors limiting the progress of higher education pedagogy. On one hand, it was difficult to persuade professionals to engage in higher education studies; on the other hand, convincing the Ministry of Education to establish research bases for each type of institution proved challenging, hindering the ability to formulate generalisations supporting the effectiveness of higher education pedagogy (Sarkadi, 1988, pp. 219–221).

Initially, the FPK focused on compiling an up-to-date bibliography of theoretical literature on higher education, publishing volumes showcasing notable foreign scientific works and documenting domestic experiences (Jáki, 1982). The state's educational policy required pedagogical expertise from different sectors, including higher education, to support the successful realisation of its goals. According to contemporary accounts and later recollections from Endre Zibolen, the FPK undertook two major initiatives to enhance their efficiency. Firstly, they conducted investigations aligned with their main research directions, involving external experts. Secondly, they organised the FPA (Sarkadi, 1988, p. 221). The Hungarian Pedagogical Society's Higher Education Section, established on April 23, 1969, also collaborated in developing the FPA program and organising lectures (Héberger, 1970; Megalakult a Magyar Pedagógiai Társaság Felsőoktatási Tagozata, 1969).

The Higher Education Pedagogical Academy

The FPA launched a lecture series on November 3, 1970, which lasted until May 9, 1972. Renowned experts, including those specialising in higher education topics, delivered monthly or bi-monthly lectures as part of this training program. Organised as a collaboration between the FPK and the Hungarian Pedagogical Society (MPT), the lectures were held during meetings of the Higher Education Section of the Hungarian Pedagogical Society. Organisers emphasised both oral and written communication, with participants recruited by means of circulars to ensure that as many people as possible were informed about the lectures. Attendees received the lecture materials in stencil form, and finalised volumes were compiled and sent to leaders of higher education institutions, as well as national and pedagogical libraries (Rathmanné, 1972). Following the lectures, participants engaged in closing discussions where they could engage in debates on various higher education issues. The venue and duration of these scientific and professional communications expanded over time. Beyond Budapest, there were nationwide efforts and demands for discussion on higher education issues, leading to similar lectures and debates organised at several universities and colleges across the country (Benedek, 1973). In a retrospective article, Éva Széchy (1983), a member involved in the organisation of the MPT, reported that hundreds of interested individuals, participants, and readers took part. However, based on the available information, it is unclear to what extent this high level of activity was driven by propaganda efforts or how it influenced subsequent collaborations, dialogues, new research, and the creation of cognitive products in the mid-1970s amidst the changing educational policy environment.

The educational and scientific elite on the stage of higher education pedagogy

In chronological order, the following 12 specialists delivered a total of 13 lectures in the series: László Kahulits, Endre Zibolen, János Farkas, László Vörös, Szilárd Faludi, Ferenc Biczók, András Tigyi, László Kelemen, Sándor Nagy, Péter Szedlay, Tibor Erdey-Grúz, István Hahn, and Éva Széchy.[3] These individuals were key professional figures who conveyed and shared their own compiled and created knowledge on higher education pedagogy. Their insights were shared to a professional audience both through their lectures and in the volumes edited by János Palovecz.

Insights can be gained from examining the impact of the personal backgrounds of this well-defined group on the formation and autonomy of higher education pedagogy. As a general observation is that the lecturers were recognised and credible experts. The literature offers several approaches to interpret and operationalize recognition; from these I have chosen to highlight two aspects from the concept of knowledge elite for this analysis: the educational and the scientific spheres (Kováts, 2011, p. 76). Members of the educational and scientific elite hold positions endowed with significant symbolic, communicative, and social capital in addition to their professional and scientific knowledge. These elements influence the institutionalisation, position, and recognition of a discipline. According to this approach, an important question arises as to whether the lecturers of the

3 See Appendix 1 for details.

FPA can be considered as members of the educational and scientific elite during their tenure at the FPA.

Given the limited scope of this study for detailed theoretical and methodological elaborations on the elite, in seeking a practical methodological answer to the above question I largely relied on the categorisation of the scientific elite laid out by Viktor Karády (2015, pp. 255–265). (For various interpretations of the elite, see, e.g., Bourdieu, 1999; Darvai, 2020; Huszár, 2006; Kováts I., 2011; Kristóf, 2011; Nagy, 2013; Németh, 2015; Pénzes, 2021.)

Education was identified as a basic criterion for membership in the knowledge elite: each lecturer at the FPA held a Hungarian university degree, with two of them, Tibor Erdey-Grúz and István Hahn, also pursuing university studies in Germany. All of them belonged to the state-sanctioned educational and scientific elite, evidenced by their teaching roles at universities and doctoral degrees. Three of them (Tibor Erdey-Grúz, László Kelemen, and Sándor Nagy) were doctors of the Hungarian Academy of Sciences (MTA), while two were corresponding and regular members of the MTA (Tibor Erdey-Grúz and István Hahn). Several could also be classified as part of the elite based on the various key positions that they held. This included ministry employees and department heads (László Kahulits and Éva Széchy), a university vice-rector (László Kelemen), department heads (István Hahn, László Kelemen, and Sándor Nagy), and institute directors (János Farkas and Endre Zibolen). The prestige of these positions was complemented and enhanced by the recognition they gained based on their internal autonomy within their respective scientific fields (e.g., good reputation, recognition, and success), of which the lecturers of the FPA possessed a considerable amount. Several of them held elected positions in various professional organisations (e.g., the Hungarian Biophysical Society; Hungarian Biochemical Society; Hungarian Pedagogical Society, MTA Committee on Educational History, and Hungarian Psychological Society), received professional awards (e.g., the Academy Award and Excellent Worker in Education), or were editors of important professional journals (e.g., *Hungarian Pedagogy*) and series (e.g., *Hungarian Pedagogical Literature*). All of the FPA lecturers can also be considered members of the elite on the basis of state and professional consensus (compare Karády, 2015, p. 257). Their membership in the knowledge elite is further reinforced by their active engagement in their respective professional fields. This includes publishing studies and books, receiving peer feedback, expressing opinions on professional matters, and maintaining international connections (albeit limited).

When examining membership in the educational and scientific elite, it is crucial to consider social conditions. After World War II, the traditional emphasis on personal excellence and merit diminished in the emerging party-state system.

In its place, political loyalty became a significant factor, as the system, following the Soviet model, favoured politically reliable candidates for inclusion into the educational and scientific elite. For example, university appointments were subject to approval by the party apparatus, and the adoption of the Soviet scientific qualification system led to the large-scale displacement of the old elite and the selection of their replacements (Karády, 2015; Nagy, 2013; Németh, 2015; Pénzes, 2021). In the late 1960s and early 1970s, a more liberal education and science policy began to influence the criteria for membership in the knowledge elite, where, alongside loyalty, educational and scientific achievements also became important. This process, marked by contradictions, saw professionals from various backgrounds influencing higher education pedagogy. Among the FPA lecturers were individuals marginalised and then readmitted after 1956 (Endre Zibolen), politically active individuals (László Kahulits and Éva Széchy), those who were active but struggling with crises (Szilárd Faludi), those who were politically less active (László Kelemen), and those committed to religion (Ferenc Biczók). This eclecticism indicates that power dynamics within the 'existing socialism' influenced education and science policy, fostering an increasingly sophisticated set of rules for representatives of the knowledge elite (Morsányi, 2009, p. 5).

We believe that the above categorisation provides a sufficient and appropriate basis to conclude that the lecturers of the FPA – taking into account the influence of the political environment – belonged to the meritocratic knowledge elite based on their qualifications, as well as their scientific and professional achievements. With their involvement, professional credibility, lectures, and publications, they played a role in sustaining interest in higher education pedagogy and in enhancing the position and social recognition of the discipline.

The appearance of higher education pedagogy in the topics of the FPA

In the late 1960s, the FPK was instrumental in the marked expansion of higher education pedagogy. Its primary aim was to involve a wide range of educators in producing a comprehensive overview of the best domestic practices and to make the most notable achievements from abroad accessible (Zibolen, 1971, pp. 45–46). In selecting the focal themes of the lecture series, emphasis was placed on selecting competitive and credible scientific contributions and practical approaches to education. The lecturers addressed the following topics and issues:

- The necessity of pedagogical awareness in higher education.
- The path to university or college, including the admissions process and the introduction of the admitted students to their studies.

- Sociological characteristics of university students.
- Psychological and pedagogical principles for modernising higher education.
- Educational characteristics in higher education.
- The complexities of the educational process.
- Teaching methods: lectures, seminars, practical sessions, the use of audiovisual aids, and examination methods.
- The relationship between research and teaching in higher education (see Appendix 1).

The above-mentioned topics reflect an effort to establish higher education pedagogy as a discipline interconnected with higher education practice. The detailed elaboration of these topics during the lectures suggests that the lecture series provided an institutional space for specialists in higher education issues to raise essential problems, and to summarize and disseminate theoretically and methodologically grounded knowledge. The lectures contributed to delineating the field of higher education pedagogy and outlining the knowledge expected from instructors in the field.

In the 1950s, the communist paradigm fundamentally restructured the institutional and cognitive elements of interpreting science (see Baska, 2015; Németh & Biró, 2016). Examining the topics and issues of the FPA lectures it becomes apparent that, alongside changes in society, a more open cultural conception of science emerged around the turn of the 1960s and 1970s. It is noteworthy that during this period, while political considerations and ideological expectations were often present in the background, there was a discernible tendency to prioritize expertise. This was manifested in the lectures, which drew not only from the Soviet model but also increasingly incorporated domestic as well as international sources and reference points, both Eastern and Western. This broader engagement reflects an orientation towards with a more inclusive and reflective approach towards scholarly discourse.

During this period of openness, institutional capacities expanded, leading to the readmission of the "bourgeois" social sciences of the 1950s, such as a more professionalised sociology, diversified psychology, and more flexible, open pedagogy (Kalmár, 2014, p. 81; Pléh, 2019, p. 133; Takács, 2016, p. 38). This expansion made it possible to establish connections between now legitimised sciences and emphasised the strengthening of interdisciplinary approaches. Interdisciplinary aspects were faintly present in the content of some of the lectures published in the FPA volumes, reflected in the sum of the lectures and writings that mirrored the pedagogical, psychological, sociological, economic, historical, organisational, and statistical perspectives and approaches. Endre Zibolen's slightly modified observation is pertinent here; noting that practitioners of the aforementioned sciences often approached their subjects not in a mono- rather than multidisciplinary manner (Zibolen, 1980, p. 391).

The lectures served as continuations of the educational knowledge content developed by the knowledge elite and made public in the late 1960s. In these sessions, the knowledge content related to higher education pedagogy became consolidated and enriched; in addition, the experts provided theoretical and practical foundations for the further development of higher education pedagogy as an independent discipline.

Summary

From the late 1960s to the early 1970s, an increasingly social atmosphere provided a favourable environment for the emancipation of higher education pedagogy. The expanding institutional structures, such as the Higher Education Pedagogy Research Centre and the Higher Education Pedagogy Academy, as well as emerging communication networks such as the *Higher Education Review*, research reports produced by the Higher Education Pedagogy Centre, various publications, and conferences, helped shape the frameworks and content of developed in this process. Some members of the knowledge elite contributed to the social recognition of the discipline by taking an active role in its cultivation. However, several conditions still needed to be met for the field to be recognised as an independent discipline, such as the establishment of further institutions within universities (e.g., institutes and departments), expanding international cooperation, the development of conceptual frameworks, and publishing textbooks. Despite the challenges encountered, this period can be considered as a phase in the development of higher education pedagogy, warranting further research and a deeper understanding of this area of research.

Bibliography

Akadémiai Almanach (1973). *A Magyar Tudományos Akadémia Almanachja.* Akadémiai Kiadó. https://real-j.mtak.hu/3091/1/Almanach_1973.pdf

A Szerkesztőség (1960). Felsőoktatásunk feladatai a Magyar Szocialista Munkáspárt VII. Kongresszusa határozatainak végrehajtásában. *Felsőoktatási Szemle*, *9*(1), 1.

Baska, G. (2015). *Rituális elemek a Rákosi-korszak pedagógiai sajtójának propaganda szövegeiben.* In G. Baska, & J. Hegedűs (Eds.), *Égi iskolák, földi műhelyek: Tanulmányok a 65 éves Németh András tiszteletére* (pp. 344–358).

Eötvös Loránd Tudományegyetem Pedagógiai és Pszichológiai Kar. https://real.mtak.hu/33283/1/nemeth_65_kotet_vegleges_u.pdf

Báthory, Z., & Falus, I. (Eds.). (1997). *Pedagógiai Lexikon* (Vol. 1–3). Keraban Könyvkiadó.

Benedek, A. (1973). Felsőoktatás külföldön. Fiatal oktatók pedagógiai képzése Európa egyetemein és főiskoláin. *Felsőoktatási Szemle, 22*(6), 377–380.

Bor, P. (1965). Nemzetközi Tudományos Ülésszak a tanárképzés pedagógiájáról a Szegedi Tanárképző Főiskolán. *Felsőoktatási Szemle, 14*(6), 400–401.

Bourdieu, P. (1999). Gazdasági tőke, kulturális tőke, társadalmi tőke. In R. Angelusz (Ed.), *A társadalmi rétegződés komponensei* (pp. 156–177). Új Mandátum Könyvkiadó.

Darvai, T. (2016). Szakmai-politikai nézetek és ideológiák az V. Nevelésügyi Kongresszuson. *Neveléstudomány | Oktatás – Kutatás – Innováció, 4*(3), 49–61. https://doi.org/10.21549/NTNY.15.2016.3.4

Elekes, L., & Zibolen, E. (1964). A szervezett felsőoktatási pedagógiai kutatómunka megindulása. *Felsőoktatási Szemle, 13* (1), 4–9.

Felsőoktatási Pedagógiai Kutatóközpont (1976). In S. Nagy (Eds.), *Pedagógiai Lexikon* (Vol. 1, p. 445). Akadémiai Kiadó.

Faludi, Sz., & Kóczy, L. (1964). A felsőoktatási didaktikai-metodikai kutatások. *Felsőoktatási Szemle, 13*(11), 650–656.

Megalakult a Magyar Pedagógiai Társaság Felsőoktatási Tagozata (1969). *Felsőoktatási Szemle, 18*(5), 303.

Geiger, R. L. (1980). The Changing Demand for Higher Education in the Seventies: Adaptations within Three National Systems. *Higher Education, 9*(3), 255–276. https://doi.org/10.1007/BF00138517

Gerhard, R. (1963). Az egyetemi oktatással és neveléssel foglalkozó kutatómunka megindulása és első eredményei a Német Demokratikus Köztársaságban. *Felsőoktatási Szemle, 12*(10), 630–636.

Halász, G. (1988). *Az oktatáspolitika alakításának állami-politikai mechanizmusai a hetvenes és a nyolcvanas évek elején.* Oktatáskutató Intézet. http://halaszg.elte.hu/download/Oktataspolitika_60-70-es_evek.htm

Hahn, I. (1970). Felsőoktatási neveléselméleti munkánk helyzete, eredményei és problémái. *Felsőoktatási Szemle, 19*(3), 146–151.

Héberger, K. (1970). A Magyar Pedagógiai Társaság Felsőoktatási Tagozatának működése. *Felsőoktatási Szemle, 19*(6), 420.

Jáki, L. (1982). A Felsőoktatási Pedagógiai Kutatóközpont kiadványairól. *Magyar Pedagógia, 82*(3), 285–286.

Jensen, D., & Freeman, S. (2019). Stepping to Center Stage: The Rise of Higher Education as a Field of Study. *The Journal of Educational Foundations, 32*(1–4), 24–48. https://files.eric.ed.gov/fulltext/EJ1240068.pdf

Kalmár, M. (2014). *Történelmi galaxisok vonzásában: Magyarország és a szovjetrendszer, 1945–1990*. Osiris Kiadó.

Karády, V. (2015). *Egy szocialista értelmiségi "államnemesség"? Kandidátusok és akadémiai doktorok a hazai társadalomtudományokban*. In A. Németh, Zs. H. Biró, & I. Garai (Eds.), *Neveléstudomány és tudományos elit a 20. század második felében* (pp. 251–281). Gondolat Kiadó. https://real.mtak.hu/35462/1/Nevelestudomany_törd_1.pdf

Kelemen, E. (2017). A Magyar Pedagógiai Társaság újjáalakulása és tevékenységének első évtizede (1967–1976). *Új Pedagógiai Szemle, 67*(9–10), 72–87. https://epa.oszk.hu/00000/00035/00183/pdf/EPA00035_upsz_2017_09-10_072-087.pdf

Kovács, I. G., & Kende, G. (2011). *A tudáselit középiskolái. A két világháború közötti tudáselit középszintű iskoláztatása 1860 és 1920 között*. In I. G. Kovács (Eds.), *Elitek és iskolák, felekezetek és etnikumok. Társadalom- és kultúratörténeti tanulmányok* (pp. 75–99). L'Harmattan.

Kozma, T. (2006). *Az összehasonlító neveléstudomány alapjai*. Új Mandátum Kiadó. https://mek.oszk.hu/08900/08963/08963.pdf

Kristóf, L. (2011). *A magyar elitértelmiség reputációja: Doktori disszertáció*. Budapesti Corvinus Egyetem Szociológia Doktori Iskola. http://phd.lib.uni-corvinus.hu/573/1/Kristof_Luca.pdf

Ladányi, A. (2000a). Zibolen Endre tevékenysége a szervezett felsőoktatás-elméleti kutatások megindítása terén. *Magyar Pedagógia, 100*(1), 105–111. https://magyarpedagogia.bibl.u-szeged.hu/index.php/magyarpedagogia/article/view/167/166

Ladányi, A. (2000b). Szervezett felsőoktatás-elméleti kutatások megindulása Magyarországon: Emlékezés Zibolen Endrére. *Educatio, 9*(1), 3–12. https://real-j.mtak.hu/16942/1/2000_1.pdf

Ladányi, A. (1999). *A magyar felsőoktatás a 20. században*. Akadémiai Kiadó.

Lipák, J. (1964). A felsőoktatási pedagógia és didaktika kidolgozásának alapelvei. *Felsőoktatási Szemle, 13*(9), 528–531.

Morsányi, B. (2009). *Magyarország és egy ifjú nemzedék a hatvanas-hetvenes évek fordulóján: A „hatvanas évek": csalóka napfény és csalóka emlékezet*. Eötvös Loránd Tudományegyetem Bölcsészettudományi Kar Irodalomtudományi Doktori Iskola. https://epika.web.elte.hu/doktor/publ_Morsanyi_B1.pdf

Némedi, L. (1960). Tanárképzésünk fejlődésének útja a felszabadulás óta. *Felsőoktatási Szemle, 9*(4), 201–205.

Németh, A. (2010). A pedagógiatörténet funkcióváltozása és annak megjelenése a hazai kutatásokban. In É. Szabolcs, & I. Garai (Eds.), *Neveléstudomány – reflexió – innováció* (pp. 149–187). Gondolat Kiadó.

Németh, A. (2015). Főbb tudományelméleti irányzatok, kutatási eredményeik és hatásuk nemzetközi és hazai neveléstudomány-tudománytörténeti kutatásokra. In A. Németh, Zs. H. Biró, & I. Garai (Eds.), *Neveléstudomány és tudományos elit a 20. század második felében* (pp. 9–83). Gondolat Kiadó. https://real.mtak.hu/35462/1/Nevelestudomany_törd_1.pdf

Németh, A., & Biró Zs. H. (2016). A magyar neveléstudomány diszciplína jellemzőinek és kognitív tartalmainak változásai a 20. század második felében. In A. Németh, I. Garai, & Z. A. Szabó (Eds.), *Neveléstudomány és pedagógiai kommunikáció a szocializmus időszakában* (pp. 7–118). Gondolat Kiadó. https://real.mtak.hu/39151/1/PTE_Nemeth_javitott.pdf

Pečenková, M. (1967). Felsőoktatás külföldön. Vysoká Škola. *Felsőoktatási Szemle, 16*(10), 639–640.

Pénzes, D. (2021). *A neveléstudományi elit átalakulása a Rákosi-korszakban: Doktori disszertáció.* Eszterházy Károly Katolikus Egyetem Neveléstudományi Doktori Iskola. https://disszertacio.uni-eszterhazy.hu/87/1/Pénzes_disszetáció.pdf

Polónyi, I. (2009). Felsőoktatás és tudománypolitika. *Educatio, 18*(1), 85–102. https://epa.oszk.hu/01500/01551/00047/pdf/913.pdf

Pléh, Cs. (2019). Intézmények és gondolkodásmódok fél évszázad magyar pszichológiájában (1960–2010) In Cs. Pléh, J. Mészáros, & V. Csépe (Eds.), *A pszichológiatörténetírás módszerei és a magyar pszichológiatörténet* (pp. 133–160). Gondolat Kiadó. https://real.mtak.hu/144835/1/PlehCsaba_Pszichologiatortenet.pdf

Rathmanné, T. M. (1972). Korszerű oktatási módszerek a felsőoktatásban. A Felsőoktatási Pedagógiai Kutatóközpont kiadványairól. *Tájékoztató, 18*(6), 228–239.

Sarkadi, L. (1988). *Beszélgetés Zibolen Endrével.* Oktatáskutató Intézet.

Schrecker, E. (2021). *The Lost Promise: American Universities in the 1960s.* University of Chicago Press.

Stichweh, R. (1994). *Wissenschaft, Universitat, Professionen.* Suhrkamp.

Stichweh, R. (1997). Professions in modern society. *International Review of Sociology, 7*(1), 95–102. https://doi.org/10.1080/03906701.1997.9971225

Széchy, É. (1983). Felújította tevékenységét a Magyar Pedagógiai Társaság Felsőoktatási Szakosztálya. *Felsőoktatási Szemle, 32*(6), 381–382.

Takács, R. (2016). A magyar kultúra nyitottsága az 1970-es években. *Múltunk – Politikatörténeti Folyóirat, 61*(4), 24–56. https://www.multunk.hu/wp-content/uploads/2017/11/takacsr_16_4.pdf

Trencsényi-Waldapfel, I. (1960). Egyetemeink bölcsészeti karainak feladatai a VII. Pártkongresszus után. *Felsőoktatási Szemle, 9*(1), 9–12.

Zibolen, E. (1964). A felsőoktatási pedagógiai kutatómunka helyzetéről. *Felsőoktatási Szemle, 13*(10), 582–586.

Zibolen, E. (1967). A régi fáklya világnál. A Magyar Pedagógiai Társaság és a felsőoktatási pedagógia. *Köznevelés, 23*(13–14), 537–538.

Zibolen, E. (1980). Jelentés a neveléstudomány helyzetéről. *Magyar Pedagógia, 80*(4), 387–398. https://real-j.mtak.hu/4794/1/MagyarPedagogia_1980.pdf

Appendix 1

Lectures and volumes of the Higher Education Pedagogical Academy

The editor of the volumes: János Palovecz.

Kahulits, L. (1970). *A felvételtől az elhelyezkedésig. Az egyetemi és főiskolai hallgatók kiválasztásának, hivatásra való felkészítésének és pályára irányításának főbb kérdései.* Felsőoktatási Pedagógiai Kutatóközpont.

Zibolen, E. (1971). *Felsőoktatás és pedagógiai tudatosság.* Felsőoktatási Pedagógiai Kutatóközpont.

Farkas J., & Vörös L. (1971). *Az egyetemi hallgató. Két tanulmány.* Felsőoktatási Pedagógiai Kutatóközpont.

Faludi, Sz. (1971). *Az előadás.* Felsőoktatási Pedagógiai Kutatóközpont.

Biczók, F. (1971). *A gyakorlat a felsőoktatásban.* Felsőoktatási Pedagógiai Kutatóközpont.

Tigyi, A. (1971). *Az objektív vizsgáztatás.* Felsőoktatási Pedagógiai Kutatóközpont.

Kelemen, L. (1971). *A felsőfokú oktatás korszerűsítésének pszichológiai alapjai.* Felsőoktatási Pedagógiai Kutatóközpont.

Nagy, S. (1971). *Újabb kutatások a felsőfokú oktatási folyamat pedagógiai vonatkozásaiban.* Felsőoktatási Pedagógiai Kutatóközpont.

Szedlay, P. (1972). *Audiovizuális eszközök a felsőoktatásban.* Felsőoktatási Pedagógiai Kutatóközpont.

Erdey-Grúz, T., & Hahn, I. (1972). *Kutatás és oktatás.* Felsőoktatási Pedagógiai Kutatóközpont.

Hahn, I. (1972). *A szemináriumvezetés módszertani kérdései.* Felsőoktatási Pedagógiai Kutatóközpont.

Széchy, É. (1972). *A nevelés rendszere fejlődésének új tendenciái a felsőoktatásban.* Felsőoktatási Pedagógiai Kutatóközpont.

Authors of the book

Zsófia Albrecht is an assistant research fellow at the Institute of Art History, Research Centre for the Humanities (HUN-REN Hungarian Research Network) and is the collections manager of the Art Collection of the Hungarian Academy of Sciences. She collaborates as a museum educator with the Hungarian National Gallery since 2011. Her PhD research at Eötvös Loránd University focuses on 19th century art education, the life reform movements and reform education.

Attila Czabaji Horváth is a Professor at the Institute of Education, Faculty of Education and Psychology, Eötvös Loránd University. After obtaining his PhD, he became a senior research fellow at the Országos Pedagógiai Intézet [National Institute of Pedagogy], where he worked on institutional development and alternative pedagogies. He has been working in higher education for 28 years, previously as Head of Department and Director General of the Teacher Training Centre at the University of Pannonia. His research focuses on Freinet pedagogy, informal learning and teacher-student relationships.

Andrea Daru is a doctoral candidate at the Doctoral School of Education, Faculty of Education and Psychology, Eötvös Loránd University. Her research focuses on life reform movements and reforms in music and art education in the early 20th century, with special emphasis on the work of Béla Bartók.

Tibor Darvai is a senior lecturer at the Eötvös Loránd University Bárczi Gusztáv Faculty of Special Needs Education (Budapest, Hungary). In his research, he analyses the connections between socialist education policy, educational science, and socialist ideology. His interests include the interdisciplinary relationship between educational science and psychology. His latest book analyses the period of Hungarian socialist education policy between 1956 and 1970, and how the educational policy views of this period were presented in the journal *A Tanító* [The Teacher] (Education policy in the early Kádár era, based on the analysis of the journal 'The Teacher').

Imre Garai is an associate professor in the Research Group for Historical, Theoretical and Comparative Pedagogy at the Institute of Education, Eötvös Loránd University. During his graduate and postgraduate studies, he was a member of the Eötvös József Collegium. In his PhD dissertation, he summarised the history of this institution. In 2020, he earned his habilitation degree about the institutional and professional development of secondary school teachers in Hungary between 1862 and 1919. He published several books and articles (including his PhD dissertation in English) about the professional development of secondary teachers. Additionally, he is also an author of papers about the development of educational sciences in Central Europe in the 19th and 20th centuries and the role of remembrance and recollection in the professional career of pedagogues.

Erzsébet Golnhofer is a retired honorary professor, habilitated associate professor, and Candidate of Sciences. She taught many pedagogical subjects at Eötvös Loránd University from 1972 onwards, and is the founder and former head of the Doctoral School of Education. Additionally, she has been working as an editor for several pedagogical journals and series. She has participated in various national and international development projects as a researcher and subject leader. Her research mainly focuses on educational theory, higher education pedagogy, and the history of education. Some of her specific research interests include adaptive education, continuity and discontinuity in the history of Hungarian education, politics and pedagogy, and the interpretations of childhood.

Emese Lukovszki is a student at at the Doctoral School of Education, Faculty of Education and Psychology, Eötvös Loránd University (ELTE). Her research interests include the history of the development of education science and the phenomenon of cyberbullying.

András Németh is a Doctor of the Hungarian Academy of Sciences, a full professor of Selye János University in Komárno (Slovakia), and a professor emeritus at the Eötvös Loránd University, Faculty of Education and Psychology in Budapest. The general and historical education, the history of life reform and models of 'new education', the history of the discipline and the history of the reception European intellectual trends in the Central European and Hungarian educational sciences stand in the focus of his research activities and research interest. His scientific activities can be accessed in details here: curriculum78.webnode.hu/

Zsuzsanna Polyák is a research fellow and lecturer at the Kodály Institute of the Ferenc Liszt Academy of Music, and she also works as an archivist. She is member of the Research Group for Historical, Theoretical and Comparative Pedagogy in the Institute of Education at Eötvös Loránd University and participates in two projects: '*Life-reform Movements and the Arts*'; and '*The Past and Present of the Hungarian Educational Science: Development of a Discipline, Scientific Communication (1970–2017)*'. Her main research area is music education history, with a special focus on the Kodály concept and its international dissemination, and past and current philosophies and ideologies in music education.

Bence Ruzsa is a PhD student at the Doctoral School of Education, Eötvös Loránd University (ELTE), and also a member of the Research Group for Historical, Theoretical and Comparative Pedagogy since 2019. In 2023, he graduated as a secondary school teacher at the ELTE Faculty of Science. His main areas of interest are the educational policy during the period of the Austro-Hungarian Empire, with special emphasis on the institutionalisation of industrial education, the party education system in the socialist period of Hungary, and the application of content analysis and prosopography to the History of Education. He is also a member of the Presidency of the Hungarian Reform-Pedagogical Association.

Lajos Somogyvári works as an associate professor at the University of Pannonia in Veszprém (Hungary); he is the head of the Institute of Education Sciences and is vice-dean responsible for scientific affairs and accreditation. His PhD thesis (2014) was a visual study of Hungarian schools in the 1960s. He has been working on educational policies, ideology, and propaganda between 1945 and 1960 in Hungary recently, including Cold War perspectives and transnational tendencies. He is the international secretary of the History of Education Subcommittee of the Hungarian Academy of Sciences, a member of the Executive Committee at the International Standing Conference for the History of Education (ISCHE) and is co-convenor at EERA Network 17. (Histories of Education).

Zoltán András Szabó is an assistant professor at Eötvös Loránd University, Faculty of Education and Psychology, Institute of Education, where he leads the Research Group for Historical, Theoretical and Comparative Education. His work includes publications on the history and current issues in public education and educational science. His primary research interest is educational discourse analysis using innovative methods, particularly computer-aided content analysis and network theory. He earned his PhD in educational science in 2017.

Dorina Szente earned her doctoral degree in 2021, following the defense of her dissertation titled "The Impact of School Rituals on Education – Especially the Development of Girls' and Women's Education in the First Half of the 20th Century". She is currently an Assistant Professor at the Hungarian University of Dance Art.

Beatrix Vincze has been a lecturer at the Eötvös Loránd University, Faculty of Pedagogy and Psychology since 2009. She is currently an associate professor and the supervisor of the undergraduate (Bachelor of Arts) program in Pedagogy and the Museum Education specialisation program, and a member of the Research Group for Historical, Theoretical and Comparative Education. Her research interests include the history of teacher training, reform pedagogy (museum pedagogy) and the life reform movements. She obtained her PhD degree in 2007, followed by her habilitation degree in 2019. She has participated in several national and international projects on the history of teacher education in the Central European region and the reception history of the reform pedagogy and life reform movements. In her publications, she focuses mainly on the context of the Hungarian reform pedagogy and life reform efforts, the historical aspects of museum pedagogy and its changes in the 21st century.

Györgyi Vincze is an Assistant Professor at Eötvös Loránd University, Bárczi Gusztáv Faculty of Special Needs Education in Budapest (Hungary). She is qualified as special needs teacher and psychologist. Previously, she worked with children with mild intellectual disability. Her research interests include teachers' perceptions of children's moral development and moral education.

Erziehung in Wissenschaft und Praxis

Herausgegeben von Johanna Hopfner und Claudia Stöckle

Band 1 Johanna Hopfner: Gelegentliche Gedanken über Erziehung. 2008.

Band 2 Johanna Hopfner / András Németh (Hrsg.): Pädagogische und kulturelle Strömungen in der k. u. k. Monarchie. Lebensreform, Herbartianismus und reformpädagogische Bewegungen. 2008.

Band 3 Agnes Trattner: Piercing, Tattoo und Schönheitsoperationen. Jugendliche Protesthaltung oder psychopathologische Auffälligkeit? Eine pädagogische Studie zum Körpererleben in der weiblichen Adoleszenz. 2008.

Band 4 Edvard Protner / Vladimir Wakounig / Robi Kroflič̌ (Hrsg.): Pädagogische Konzeptionen zwischen Vergangenheit und Zukunft. Ambivalenzen, Begriffsverwirrungen und Reformeifer. 2009.

Band 5 Johanna Hopfner / András Németh / Éva Szabolcs (Hrsg.): Kindheit – Schule – Erziehungswissenschaft in Mitteleuropa 1948–2008. 2009.

Band 6 Claudia Gerdenitsch: Erst kommt die Ästhetik, dann kommt die Moral. Bedingungen der Möglichkeit von Moralerziehung. 2010.

Band 7 Attila Nóbik / Béla Pukánszky (Hrsg.): Normalität, Abnormalität und Devianz. Gesellschaftliche Konstruktionsprozesse und ihre Umwälzungen in der Moderne. 2010.

Band 8 Claudia Gerdenitsch / Johanna Hopfner (Hrsg./eds.): Erziehung und Bildung in ländlichen Regionen – Rural Education. 2011.

Band 9 András Németh / Ehrenhard Skiera (Hrsg.): Lehrerbildung in Europa. Geschichte, Struktur und Reform. 2012.

Band 10 Edvard Protner: Herbartianism and its Educational Consequences in the Period of the Austro-Hungarian Monarchy. The Case of Slovenia. 2014.

Band 11 András Németh / Claudia Stöckl / Beatrix Vincze (eds./Hrsg.): Survival of Utopias – Weiterlebende Utopien. Life Reform and Progressive Education in Austria and Hungary – Lebensreform und Reformpädagogik in Österreich und Ungarn. 2017.

Band 12 Barbara Šteh, Janko Muršak, Jasna Mažgon, Jana Kalin and Mrvar Gregorčič: School – Home – Community: Inevitable Connections. 2018.

Band 13 Beatrix Vincze / Katalin Kempf / András Németh (eds.): Hidden Stories – the Life Reform Movements and Art. 2020.

Band 14 Simonetta Polenghi / András Németh / Tomáš Kasper (eds.): Education and the Body in Europe (1900–1950) – Movement, public health, pedagogical rules and cultural ideas. 2021.

Band 15 Claudia Stöckl / Agnes Trattner (Hrsg.): Erziehen in einer unübersichtlich gewordenen Welt. Positionen, Widersprüche, Utopien 2020.

Band 16 Evelina Scaglia (ed.): Giuseppe Lombardo Radice in the early 20th century. A rediscovery of his pedagogy. 2023.

Band 17 Zoltán András Szabó / Lajos Somogyvári / Imre Garai / András Németh (eds.): Evolving perspectives. The development of Hungarian educational science after 1945. 2025.

www.peterlang.com

www.ingramcontent.com/pod-product-compliance
Lightning Source LLC
Chambersburg PA
CBHW070922150426
42812CB00049B/1363

* 9 7 8 3 6 3 1 9 1 0 1 6 0 *